Dietrich Bonhoeffer's
Christmas Sermons

OTHER BOOKS IN THIS SERIES

Dietrich Bonhoeffer's
Christmas Sermons

Editor and Translator
Edwin Robertson

ZONDERVAN™

GRAND RAPIDS, MICHIGAN 49530 USA

ZONDERVAN™

Dietrich Bonhoeffer's Christmas Sermons
Copyright © 2005 by Edwin Robertson
Previously published in the UK as *I Stand at the Door*

Requests for information should be addressed to:

Zondervan, *Grand Rapids, Michigan 49530*

Library of Congress Cataloging-in-Publication Data

Bonhoeffer, Dietrich, 1906-1945.
    [Sermons. English. Selections]
    Dietrich Bonhoeffer's Christmas sermons / editor and translator, Edwin
Robertson.
       p. cm.
    Includes bibliographical references (p.   ).
    ISBN-13: 978-0-310-25955-8
    ISBN-10: 0-310-25955-X
    1. Advent sermons. 2. Christmas sermons. 3. Sermons, German—
Translations into English. I. Title: Christmas sermons. II. Title.
BV4254.5.B68 2005
252'.61—dc22

2005017160

This edition printed on acid-free paper.

Interior design by Beth Shagene

Printed in the United States of America

---

05 06 07 08 09 10 /❖ DCI/ 13 12 11 10 9 8 7 6 5 4 3

Contents

*And then, Advent comes. So many beautiful memories we
share of that season. You were the first to open up for me
the world of its music, which we have played together year
after year during the Advent weeks. A prison cell is like our
situation in Advent: one waits, hopes, does this and that—
meaningless acts—but the door is locked and can only be
opened from the outside. That is how I feel just now.*

from a letter written from his prison cell
in Tegel to Eberhard Bethge, November 21, 1943

Acknowledgments

I MUST FIRST OF ALL THANK Prof. Dr. Christian Gremmels, President of the International Bonhoeffer Society (German Section) for his encouragement, many helpful comments, and for checking the German original in the Standard Edition of Bonhoeffer's *Works* (Bonhoeffer *Werke*). The revised edition of Bethge's Biography of Bonhoeffer in English, edited by Victoria Barnett (*Dietrich Bonhoeffer: A Biography* by Eberhard Bethge, revised edition, Fortress Press, Minneapolis, 2000) has been invaluable. When I edited the first edition in 1967, I was unable to include the whole of the original German in translation. This full edition has made my work much lighter. Although I have included only one letter to his fiancée, Maria von Wedemeyer, I am grateful to Ruth-Alice von Bismarck and Ulrich Kabitz for publishing the letters to Maria and the background in *Brautbriefe Zelle 92* (Beck, 1992) and to John Brownjohn for his excellent translation into English, published as *Love Letters from Cell 92*, (Harper-Collins, 1994).

Finally, my thanks to the staff of Eagle Publishing Ltd. and especially to my editor, David Wavre, who have nursed the book through from my manual typewriter to the present form.

Edwin Robertson

Introduction

THERE IS MORE TO DIETRICH BONHOEFFER than the sound bites of *religionless Christianity*, *secular holiness*, or *man come of age*. It was unfortunate that he was introduced to the wider public by John Robinson in his influential paperback *Honest to God*, and later associated with the "Death of God" School. A better understanding of Dietrich Bonhoeffer would have recognized that, in the first place, he was a believer with a personal conviction of salvation in Christ and a sense of the importance of the church. He was a man with a deeply spiritual life.

Dietrich Bonhoeffer (1906–45) was a distinguished German theologian, but when he had to make the choice between an academic career and that of a preacher, he chose to be ordained for the pastoral office. And that ordination, in his view, was a call to preaching:

> The ministry of preaching constitutes the church's ministry rather than the office of pastor. The ministry of preaching is intrinsic and remains such; the office of pastor is a specialized division of the ministry of preaching. Ordination is the call to a preaching ministry and not primarily to the office of pastor. The commission to preach continues to be mine even if I am separated from the pastoral task within a

congregation. The ministry of preaching is an endur-
ing commission from which a person cannot free
himself after ordination.[1]

In a divided church, he opposed the so-called "German Christians" who accepted and approved of the
Hitler regime. His opposition to them was clearly stated
against the custom of many German-Christian pastors
who put a portrait of Hitler on the altar: "We have only
one altar in the church and that is to the Most High
Lord, to whom all honor and worship belongs. We have
no second altar for the honoring of men" (in a sermon
preached by Bonhoeffer in Berlin, February 26, 1933).
Because of this opposition and his outspoken condemnation of the treatment of the Jews, he was "separated
from the pastoral task within a congregation." But he
continued to preach until that was also forbidden him.
When he could not preach in public, he circulated his sermons and sermon notes to those who could use them.
Even in prison he preached in his letters, written sermons, and poems. At the last, "A Prisoner Awaiting Sentence," he preached the day before his death on the texts
"By his wounds we are healed" (Isaiah 53:5), and "Praise
be to the God and Father of our Lord Jesus Christ! In his
great mercy he has given us new birth into a living hope
through the resurrection of Jesus Christ from the dead,
and into an inheritance that can never perish, spoil or
fade—kept in heaven for you" (1 Peter 1:3,4).

We do not have the text of that sermon, but it is not difficult to imagine the relevance of his preaching to prisoners facing almost certain death. The prisoners in another room tried to smuggle him into their room that they too might worship with him and hear his sermon. Before that could happen, the door was opened and two civilians called out, "Prisoner Bonhoeffer, get ready and come with us." He was taken to Flossenburg and there, after a summary trial, was hanged in the early hours of Monday morning, April 9, 1945, with the sound of the American guns in the distance, not very far away. Preaching was the essence of Bonhoeffer's witness and no season was more important to him than the Advent season leading up to Christmas. He took every opportunity to preach at Advent. During his two years in prison before his execution, Bonhoeffer kept the festivals of the Church and none more readily than Advent with its music ringing in his ears.

The Prime Significance of Preaching

In 1925, when Bonhoeffer was nineteen and still a theological student in Berlin, he began working with Sunday school children in the local parish church where the family lived. He was immediately successful. Eberhard Bethge, his official biographer, writes: "Bonhoeffer preached to the children in his group as much as possible. He made biblical stories as exciting as sagas or as appealing as fairy tales. He went to great trouble to hold the children's attention, which is why he so carefully wrote out in advance what he proposed to tell them."[2]

He was not beyond using stories other than biblical if they made the point. He was a superb storyteller and the children loved it. One story, mentioned by Eberhard Bethge, was of an old woman shut out in the cold on a snowy night, with the door locked against her. He used this to illustrate the Advent message.

From Sunday school to prison cell, Bonhoeffer never forgot that locked door, at Advent especially. Locked to keep the Savior out, or to keep the Christian waiting inside.

It was however in the afterglow of Easter that the door opened for him on April 9, 1945, when he walked naked to his cruel death, with his last words, "This is the end— but for me the beginning of life."

Translating the Sermons

Bonhoeffer wrote out what he proposed to say in every sermon, but he did not read the script. I have borne this in mind when translating the text he left us. There are times when a literal translation would not communicate in preaching. I have, therefore, translated freely, bringing out his meaning, but not necessarily reproducing every sentence in its written form. I have used what Eugene Nida of the Bible Societies called "dynamic equivalent." Where he has quoted a line from a German hymn, for example, I have not translated, but substituted a familiar line in an English hymn.

Barcelona

March 1928 — February 1929

ON FEBRUARY 15, 1928, Bonhoeffer was appointed assistant pastor to the German-speaking congregation in Barcelona. He left the children reluctantly, but looked forward to the opportunity of regular preaching. He had become very close to the children. In his diary in Barcelona he wrote:

> On January 21, 1928 we had our last children's service. I spoke on the man sick with palsy, and particularly on the saying, "Your sins are forgiven you," and tried yet again to reveal the kernel of our gospel to the children. They were attentive and perhaps affected a little ... For some time, the congregational prayer has often sent cold shivers down my spine, but when the throng of children with whom I have spent two years prayed for me, the effect was incomparably greater.[1]

The Parish in Barcelona

Bonhoeffer suffered a culture shock when he began to meet the people of his first parish. He was the assistant minister, under Dr. Olbricht. This senior minister was well liked by his congregation, whom he did not trouble much apart from Sunday services and pastoral visits. He enjoyed their privileged company. It was left to the young assistant to start Sunday school work and even weeknight meetings for lectures. The shock was to discover the complacency of these businessmen and even their children. In a letter to his grandmother in June, contrasting the youth of Berlin with the youth of Barcelona's German community, he wrote:

> They know little or nothing of the war, revolution, and the painful aftermath of these things, they live well and comfortably, the weather is always fine—how could it be otherwise? The Youth Movement period in Germany passed by without a trace here.[2]

All the young people seemed to assume that they would continue in their fathers' businesses and took this comfortable way of life for granted. The restless young pastor was soon stirring things up—not always to the approval of his senior. But it was preaching that concerned Bonhoeffer most. He had to get to know the country, the people, their problems, and their needs. He found himself spending a great deal of time preparing his sermons and writing them out in full.

"Writing sermons still takes up a great deal of my time," he wrote to his parents, "I work on them the entire week, devoting some time to them every day." Still, he was always pleased when the minister turned the pulpit over to him. "On the first Sunday in Advent I shall be able to preach again because Olbricht will not be returning until the following week, and I am very pleased about that."[3]

This is the sermon with which the present collection begins.

December 2, 1928

Advent Sunday

"I stand at the door and knock" (Revelation 3:20).

Celebrating Advent means learning how to wait. Waiting is an art which our impatient age has forgotten. We want to pluck the fruit before it has had time to ripen. Greedy eyes are soon disappointed when what they saw as luscious fruit is sour to the taste. In disappointment and disgust they throw it away. The fruit, full of promise rots on the ground. It is rejected without thanks by disappointed hands.

The blessedness of waiting is lost on those who cannot wait, and the fulfillment of promise is never theirs. They want quick answers to the deepest questions of life and miss the value of those times of anxious waiting, seeking with patient uncertainties until the answers come. They lose the moment when the answers are revealed in dazzling clarity.

Who has not felt the anxieties of waiting for the declaration of friendship or love? The greatest, the deepest, the most tender experiences in all the world demand patient waiting. This waiting is not in emotional turmoil, but gently growing, like the emergence of spring, like God's laws, like the germinating of a seed.

Not all can wait—certainly not those who are satisfied, contented, and feel that they live in the best of all possible worlds! Those who learn to wait are uneasy about their way of life, but yet have seen a vision of greatness in the world of the future and are patiently expecting its fulfillment. The celebration of Advent is possible only to those who are troubled in soul, who know themselves to be poor and imperfect, and who look forward to something greater to come. For these, it is enough to wait in humble fear until the Holy One himself comes down to us, God in the child in the manger. God comes. The Lord Jesus comes. Christmas comes. Christians rejoice!

In a few weeks we shall hear that cry of triumph. But already we can hear in the distance the sound of the angels' song praising God and promising peace on earth. But, not so quick! It is still in the distance. It calls us to learn to wait and to wait aright.

When once again Christmas comes and we hear the familiar carols and sing the Christmas hymns, something happens to us, and a special kind of warmth slowly encircles us. The hardest heart is softened. We recall our own childhood. We feel again how we then felt, especially if we were separated from a mother. A kind of homesickness comes over us for past times, distant places, and yes, a blessed longing for a world without violence or hardness of heart. But there is something more—a longing for the safe lodging of the everlasting Father. And that leads our thoughts to the curse of homelessness which hangs heavily over the world. In every land, the endless wandering without purpose or destination. Looking beyond our own comfort here, we see in many lands people dying of cold in wintry conditions. The plight of such people disturbs us within and amidst our enjoyment; a thousand eyes look at us and the evil haunts us. Poverty and distress throughout the world worries us, but it cannot be brushed away and there appears to be nothing we can do about it.

On this first Sunday of Advent, the two inescapable realities, which have been the subject of our thoughts over the last two Sundays, with which the Christian year ended, greet us now in this first Sunday of the new year. They weigh heavily upon our souls this day: sin and death. Who can bring help as we face these destructive realities? Who can deliver us from their dire effect? Only One! Our Lord delivers us from sin and death. Shall we not cry, as the first believers did, "Come Lord!" This is the ancient cry, "Maranatha," and quickly come!

Soon we shall acknowledge that our Lord Jesus Christ comes into our world, into our homelessness, into our sin, and into our death.

Lord Jesus, come yourself, and dwell with us, be human as we are, and overcome what overwhelms us. Come into the midst of my evil, come close to my unfaithfulness. Share my sin, which I hate and which I cannot leave. Be my brother, Thou Holy God. Be my brother in the kingdom of evil and suffering and death. Come with me in my death, come with me in my suffering, come with me as I struggle with evil. And make me holy and pure, despite my sin and death.

Every day, a quiet voice answers our cry, gently, persuasively, "I stand at the door and knock."

Should we tremble at these words, this voice? The Spirit that we have called for, the Spirit that saves the world, is already here, at the door, knocking, patiently waiting for us to open the door. He has been there a long time and he has not gone away. His is a very quiet voice and few hear it. The cries of the marketplace and of those who sell shoddy goods are all too loud. But the knocking goes on and, despite the noise, we hear it at last. What shall we do? Who is it? Are we afraid or impatient? Perhaps we feel a little fear, lest someone undesirable is at the door, dangerous or with malignant intent. Should we open? In all this fuss, the royal visitor stands patiently, unrecognized, waiting. He knocks again, quite softly. Can you hear him?

And each of you may ask: Do you mean he is knocking at my door? Yes. First quiet those loud voices and listen carefully. Perhaps he knocks at the door of your heart. He wants to make your heart his own, to win your love. He would be a quiet guest within you. Jesus knocks—for you and for me. It takes only a willing ear to hear his knocking. Jesus comes, for sure, he comes again this year, and he comes to you.

When the first Christians talked of the second coming of the Lord Jesus, they thought of a great day of judgment. That seems far removed from our thoughts of Christmas, but what the early Christians thought must be taken seriously. Surely it is true still that when we hear the knock of Jesus on the door, it smites our conscience. We fear that we are not ready for him. Is our heart ready for his visit? Is it fit to be his dwelling? The dwelling place of God?

Perhaps, after all, Advent is a time for self-examination before we open the door. When we stop to consider, the contrast between those early Christians and us is extraordinary. They trembled at the thought of God coming, of the day of the Lord, when Jesus, "Judge eternal, throned in splendor," would shatter the complacency of all the world. But we take the thought of God coming among us so calmly. It is all the more remarkable when we remember that we so often associate the signs of God in the world with human suffering, the cross on Golgotha. Perhaps we have thought so much of God as love eternal and we feel the warm pleasures of Christmas when he comes gently like a child. We have been shielded from the awful nature of Christmas and no longer feel afraid at the coming near of God Almighty. We have selected from the

Christmas story only the pleasant bits, forgetting the awesome nature of an event in which the God of the universe, its Creator and Sustainer, draws near to this little planet, and now speaks to us. The coming of God is not only a message of joy, but also fearful news for anyone who has a conscience.

It is only by facing up to the fearfulness of the event that we can begin to understand the incomparable blessing. God comes into the midst of evil and death, to judge the evil in the world—and in us. And while he judges us, he loves us, he purifies us, he saves us, and he comes to us with gifts of grace and love. He makes us happy as only children know. He is, and always will be now, with us in our sin, in our suffering, and at our death. We are no longer alone. God is with us and we are no longer homeless. A piece of the eternal home is grafted into us. For that reason, we grown-ups can rejoice with all our heart around the Christmas tree—perhaps even more so than the children. We can see already the abundance of God's gifts. Just remember all the good things he has given us in the past year and, looking at this wondrous tree, feel secure in the promise of the wondrous home— the "safe lodging"—he has prepared for us. Yes, Jesus comes both with law and grace. Listen again, "Behold I stand at the door and knock." Open the door wide! How often have you thought that to see Jesus would be marvelous, that you would give everything you have to know

that he was with you. Of course, you want more than to
have him within you, you want him visible and in bod-
ily form. But how can that be? Jesus knew that his followers would want to see him and have him by them in
human form. But how can this be? He told a parable
about this—the scene of the last judgment when he
would divide the nations as a shepherd divides his sheep
from the goats.

He said to those who were truly his flock of sheep, on
his right hand:

> Come you who are blessed by my Father ... I was
> hungry and you gave me something to eat, I was
> thirsty and you gave me something to drink, I was a
> stranger and you invited me in, I needed clothes and
> you clothed me, I was sick and you looked after me, I
> was in prison and you came to visit me.

When those on his right hand asked in surprise,
"When? Where?," he answered, "I tell you the truth,
whatever you did for one of the least of these brothers
of mine, you did for me" (Matthew 25: 34–40).

With that we face the shocking reality. Jesus stands at
the door and knocks. He asks for help in the form of a
beggar, a down-and-out, a man in ragged clothes, someone who is sick, even a criminal in need of our love. He
meets you in every person you encounter in need. So long
as there are people around, Christ walks the earth as your
neighbor, as the one through whom God calls to you,

demands of you, makes claims upon you. That is the great seriousness of the Advent message and its great blessing. Christ stands at the door. He lives in the form of people around us. Will you therefore leave the door safely locked for your protection, or will you open the door for him?

It may seem odd to us that we can see Jesus in so familiar a face. But that is what he said.

Whoever refuses to take seriously this clear Advent message cannot talk of the coming of Christ into his heart. Whoever has not learned from the coming of Christ that we are all brothers and sisters in Christ, has not understood the meaning of his coming.

Christ knocks! It is not yet Christmas. And neither is it yet the great last Advent, the second coming of Christ. Through all the Advents of our life, we shall wait and look forward with longing for that day of the Lord, when God says, "I am making everything new!" (Rev 21:5). Advent is a time of waiting. Our whole life is a time of waiting; waiting for the time when there will be a new heaven and a new earth. Then all people will be as brothers and sisters, rejoicing in the words of the angels' song: "Glory to God in the highest, and on earth peace to men on whom his favor rests" (Luke 2:14).

Learn to wait! For he has promised to come: "Behold, I stand at the door." But now we call to him: "Yes, come quickly, Lord Jesus. Amen."[4]

The American Year

1929 – 1930

BONHOEFFER WAS INVITED TO REMAIN ANOTHER YEAR in Barcelona, but did not accept. This was not the kind of church work that he wanted to do. He missed the activities of a Berlin parish with its Bible study groups, youth work, lectures, and outreach. He was also a little uncertain about whether he would choose an academic career or a parish. On February 17, 1929 he was home again in Berlin-Grunewald—covered in snow.

He never forgot the Spanish culture and returned whenever there was reason. He also visited other Spanish speaking countries. One abiding interest he carried with him for the rest of his life was the story of Don Quixote and Sancho Pansa. He became acquainted with the story early one afternoon in Barcelona, when he was a little tired of his work and went to the cinema, yet what he saw was an overly long and rather poor film about Don Quixote (February 28, 1928).[1]

Even so, his passion for the story emerged and in prison towards the end of his life, he could still write to his fiancée, Maria Wedemeyer, urging her to read it, as a book that he loved.[2]

In Berlin, Bonhoeffer found the preparations for the pastorate restrictive and evaded them by returning to the university for his post-doctoral studies. Having completed these and qualifying as a university teacher, he was ordained (as he would say, "to the ministry of preaching"). Two ways were still open to him. After some consideration he applied for an exchange scholarship to Union Theological Seminary in New York. That decision gave him another year to think about the direction he wanted to take.

While studying in New York, he found the seminary close to Riverside Church on the one hand and the suburb of Harlem on the other. Harlem was, and is, populated largely by African Americans. Among the close friends he continued to correspond with long after he left America and far into the dark days of the Nazi regime in Germany were four men he had met in New York—two Europeans and two Americans. One of the Americans was African American, Frank Fisher. He introduced Bonhoeffer to Harlem and the "Ethiopian Church," where he began working in the Sunday school and was very soon much more at home among these African Americans than in the respectable white church at Riverside. In his report on America, which he titled, "Protestantism without Reformation," he wrote of the popularity of "Negro spirituals" and the applause which "Negro" singers received, but how they would not be admitted to social amenities with "whites." He explains the development of black churches and adds, "here the gospel of Jesus Christ, the Savior of the sinner, is readily preached and accepted with great welcome and visible emotion . . . Nowhere is revival preaching still so vigorous and so widespread as among the Negroes."[3]

The Visit to Cuba

During Christmas time in 1930, Bonhoeffer and his friend Erwin Sutz left New York and traveled to Cuba. The purpose was to visit Kathe Horn, his childhood governess, who was teaching at a German school in Havana. He visited her class and accepted an invitation to preach at the German-speaking church there, where he found a congregation very similar to that he had ministered to in Barcelona.

December 21, 1930 — Cuba
Advent IV—Christmas Sunday

On that same day the Lord told Moses, "Go up into the Abarim Range to Mount Nebo in Moab, across from Jericho, and view Canaan, the land I am giving the Israelites as their own possession. There on the mountain that you have climbed you will die and be gathered to your people, just as your brother Aaron died on Mount Hor and was gathered to his people. This is because both of you broke faith with me in the presence of the Israelites at the waters of Meribah Kadesh in the Desert of Zin and because you did not uphold my holiness among the Israelites. Therefore, you will see the land only from a distance; you will not enter the land I am giving to the people of Israel.'

Deut. 32:48–52

This pronouncement was a very serious matter. But Advent is a serious matter too, and indeed a terribly serious matter. We are a strange people. As Advent comes around again, we will probably sing a few Christmas carols at home with our children, rush around to buy all of our gifts, write a few Christmas cards, and then when all the office parties are over, we shall enter into the land of fun and laughter, the land of Christmas. But Moses died on the mountain, within sight of the Promised Land, able to greet it only from a distance. In the Bible, when God speaks of promises, then it is about both life and death. When we speak about promises during Advent, it is usually the promise of a few happy days with our families.

God said to Moses: "Go up into the Abarim Range and die on the mountain within sight of the Promised Land." And Moses was God's prophet, the man he had chosen to lead his people out of the house of bondage, out of the pain and suffering, into freedom. He was privileged, as he showed forth the majesty of God, striking water from the crevice in the rock. Amidst the thunders of Sinai he had brought the stone tablets of the Law to a faithless people. Since God had called him, he had no other mission than to lead the people to God's Promised Land. His life was a journey to that promise, a journey in hope, through disappointments, weariness, and despair, with grumbling and faithlessness all around him on the way. But what drove him on again and again was the hunger in him for the Promised Land. And now he is old. And only one thing sustained him and kept him going— God's word of promise, the Promised Land. He is all hope. And then at last comes the moment when all is to be fulfilled. All that he until then had believed would now be achieved, his dream come true. And now we read in the simplest words: "The Lord spoke with Moses that day ... And Moses died according to the word of the Lord."

Is it not true that that is uncomfortably serious? We know from our everyday life what unfulfilled little hopes mean. We can all give examples, and so can our children. Some of us perhaps also know of unfulfilled greater hopes. I mean hopes that are really of value, hopes to become a better person, to overcome weaknesses, to do away with secret sins. How many despairing attempts have we made, how fervently we have prayed in our distress and how hard it is when our prayers are not answered. Paul earnestly beseeched God to take away his "thorn in the flesh." But he was answered with, "Let my grace be sufficient for you" (see 2 Cor. 12:9). Live in hope and die in hope. Fulfillment is denied us. When we recall such times in our own lives, we can begin to see already how serious these words in the Bible are.

But it becomes even more uncomfortable. Why must Moses die in sight of the promise? Here we begin to see how important all these words are in the Bible: disobedience, unholy, sin, death. We no longer see that these words belong together. Sin must die before the promise is fulfilled. Moses belongs to his people, therefore he dies. If we had written the story, we would have let Moses enter the Promised Land first with great jubilation. But God says: "Go up the mountain and die." He had hoped and believed. He had a longing for a homeland he had never seen ... Jesus says: "Blessed are those who hunger and thirst for righteousness, for they will be filled." (Matthew 5:6). But Moses died on the mountain in sight of the Promise. The language of these old stories is clear enough. He who has seen God must die. Before the promise the sinner must die. Do we understand what that means for us so shortly before Christmas? Christmas will be the fulfillment of God's great promise, a promise infinitely greater than the promise of the Promised Land. God has promised to draw near to earth himself, to draw near to us; he has promised himself to lead us to deliverance, to salvation, to blessedness. But we know that if Moses had to die, we too must surely die if God deals with us according to what we deserve. But as Christians we know that we shall not die, but live in the promise, that the promise shall be life to us. But of ourselves we cannot avoid first climbing up the mountain with Moses and with courage await the word of God. Die on the mountain. Die at Advent.

You should no longer see the fulfillment. Who could go, without fear, walking confidently into the Promised Land? Perhaps children may. We can no longer do that. When we face this fact, the seriousness of the Advent season becomes clear. Great things are promised and they are in process. Unheard of happenings were proclaimed, which the ears of men have never known. Hidden secrets will be revealed. The earth and all that lives upon it will tremble at their coming. And the voice of a prophet will be heard by an anxious world, crying out, "The kingdom of heaven is at hand. God himself comes, the Lord God, Creator and Judge. He comes near, in love with humankind. He will bring them home to eternal happiness! He comes. Are you ready?"

There lies the shattering question with which the New Testament begins and ends, the only decisive question for the whole world and for the whole of our life: Are you ready for God? That is how the Bible sees the world. Watch, be awake! It is night and you want to sleep. But in the middle of the night the glory of God will be revealed. And did it not happen like that in Bethlehem? Keep your lamps burning and your loins girt or the Lord will come and woe to that servant whom he finds sleeping (Luke 12: 35–40).

It is understandable that in the middle of the night we should be tired and our eyes close in sleep. But, nonetheless, fill your lamps with oil, that if the bridegroom comes you can go to meet him. Dress yourself with party clothes, lest you be shut out from the feast of the kingdom.

So the whole of the message of Advent becomes an urgent sermon, calling men and women to repentance. Before Jesus came John the Baptist, and we must not overlook him. For the whole of the early Christians, Advent was a time for repentance, not for rejoicing. All the hymns that we have sung speak of this and it seems to me that it is right that we should have sung with repentant hearts.

(But now it is true that in three days, Christmas will come once again. The great transformation will once again happen. God would have it so. Out of the waiting, hoping, longing world, a world will come in which the promise is given. All crying will be stilled. No tears shall flow. No lonely sorrow shall afflict us anymore, or threaten. The One who helps us is there. He, who never leaves us alone, is there).

"Let us work out our salvation with fear and trembling" (Phil. 2:12).

For all that, the Bible is full of assertions that the great miracle has happened without human help, by the action of God alone. According to the most holy decision in the heavens, the Son came from the Father and at the same moment a baby was born in Bethlehem. A little child was born in a stable with the ox and the ass and a few shepherds in the fields celebrating the first Christmas. But above this stable the heavens opened and angels and stars rejoiced on that holy night. And God's love was showered upon this child. On that Christmas Day, God himself decorated the Christmas tree! The decorations were the stars of the eternal Father in heaven.

What had happened? God had looked upon the poor of the world and had himself come to help. Now he was there, not as the Almighty One, but in the seclusion of humanity. Wherever there are sinners, the weak, the sorrowful, the poor in the world, that is where God goes. Here he lets himself be found by everyone. And this message goes throughout the world, year after year anew. And it also comes once again to us this year.

We all come with different personal feelings to the Christmas festival. One comes with pure joy as he looks forward to this day of rejoicing, of friendships renewed, and of love. That is true of most children. Others look for a moment of peace under the Christmas tree, peace from the pressures of daily work. They want to dream of times and days long past. They want to forget all the unpleasant happenings around them and see the world only in the light of the Christmas tree; they want to hear the old Christmas carols. They long for this blessed forgetfulness. Others again approach Christmas with great apprehension. It will be no festival of joy for them. Personal sorrow is painful especially on this day for those whose loneliness is deepened at Christmas time. Human hearts feel emotions under the lights of the Christmas tree in so many different ways. And it is surely right that each of us should look around at the outside world for a while. Perhaps, this year, something wonderful will occur that will help us to celebrate Christmas. Before our eyes stand the crowds of the unemployed, the millions of children throughout the world in hunger and distress, the hunger in China, the oppressed in India, and those in our own unhappy land. All eyes tell us of helplessness and despair. And despite it all, Christmas comes. Whether we wish it or not, whether we are sure or not, we must hear the words once again: Christ the Savior is here! The world that Christ comes to save is our fallen and lost world. None other.[4]

[At this point the manuscript breaks off.]

The reader may speculate about how the words continued and there are enough clues in the text to write an ending. But the more significant matter is the way the preaching text, Deuteronomy 32:48–52, remained with Bonhoeffer for the rest of his life. It was prophetic of his own life-experience. In the last months of his imprisonment, his longest poem, "The Death of Moses," was composed. By then death was almost certainly near. Tightly constricted by his imposed rhyme, he ended the poem with the following lines:

Wonderfully have you dealt with me,
blends of bitterness and sweet to see,

let me through the veil of death behold,
my people at their festival bold.

God, into your eternities going,
I see my people march with freedom glowing.

You who punish sin and forgive readily,
God, you know I have loved this people steadily.

That I have borne their shame and sacrifice
and seen their salvation—will suffice.

Hold, support me, I lose my stave,
faithful God, prepare me for my grave.[5]

The war was moving to a close and the monstrous tyranny was falling when Bonhoeffer was executed.

Berlin

October 1931 – July 1933

WHILE HE WAS IN New York, letters from family and friends kept Bonhoeffer well informed about the worsening situation in Berlin: a society moving towards social, political, and economic chaos. One third of Germany's workforce was unemployed, inflation was rampant, and the Nazis were in the ascendancy. Hitler had inspired the youth of the nation. He had called for sacrifice, for subordination of the individual to the needs of the people as a whole. To eager students and young people from the poorest sections of the population alike, he held out a dream of a great Germany. Instead of humiliation which was all ten years of democracy had brought, he would make Germany great as she had once been. "You, as an individual, are nothing," he said, "the people as a whole (*Volk*) is everything." The majority of the youth of Germany followed their leader as he pointed the way to greatness. First, this meant destroying the influence of the Jews and removing them from all offices of significance in the land.

Bonhoeffer returned from America and was soon actively engaged in academic work, lecturing in the university and working within the church. He saw the need to concentrate upon the youth of Germany, whether they were university students or from the poorest suburbs of Berlin. He took over a confirmation class in Wedding, a deprived suburb, and developed a profound relationship of trust with boys from impoverished homes. He accepted the offer to become a youth secretary of the "World Alliance for International Friendship through the Churches," traveling widely in central Europe and meeting Christian youth from many places.

An Evangelical Experience

In 1931, something happened which changed Bonhoeffer radically. Looking back, he described this as the only major change that had taken place in his otherwise steadily developing life. Several of his friends noticed the change at the time, but it was to a close associate that he explained it himself, just a few years after it happened. A selection from that long account is enough to show what it meant at the time.

> Something happened that transformed my life and has remained with me to this day. For the first time, I discovered the Bible. I had often preached, had a great deal to do with the church, spoken about it, and urged support—but I had not yet become a Christian. I now know that at the time before this happened I had used the doctrine of Jesus Christ partly to my own advantage. I pray to God that that may never happen again. Also, I had never really prayed, or had done so only occasionally. For all my loneliness, I was rather pleased with myself. Then the Bible and particularly the Sermon on the Mount freed me from that. Since

then, everything has changed. It was a great liberation. I saw clearly that the life of a servant of Jesus Christ must belong to the church, and gradually I learned how far that must go. Then came the crisis of 1933. I was strengthened in my resolve by it and had found others who shared this conviction with me. The revival of the church and the ministry became my supreme concern. Now, my calling is quite clear to me. What God will make of it I do not know, but I must follow the path. Perhaps it will not be such a long one. (A letter from Finkenwald, January 27, 1936)[1]

Preaching

In New York, he had lectured and given talks and worked in the Sunday school in Harlem, but he had hardly preached at all during his year there. The one exception was the Advent sermon he gave in Cuba.

Now he began to preach again. He did not have his own pulpit, and his academic work as well as his travel prevented him from preaching every Sunday. In fact, during the two years in Berlin (1931–1933), he preached only fifteen times.

There was only one Advent sermon during this period—on November 29, 1931. Though he had no preaching engagement during the Advent season of 1932, Bonhoeffer gave a very significant devotional talk on

December 1, 1932 which recalled some of his meetings with young people in Europe as Youth Secretary of the World Alliance. In this case, he had met with French and German youth. I have included as much of the text of that talk as survived with this Advent sermon.

Bonhoeffer found itinerant preaching strange at first. His only experience of regular preaching had been in Barcelona, where he knew the congregation, and that was more or less the same each Sunday. He lived among them, visited them, arranged lectures for them, and worked in the Sunday school with their children. Now he was more or less an itinerant preacher. He preached in Trinity Church when invited by the incumbent who was also a fellow student chaplain. Often it was not for the main service of the day, but an evening service. Gerhard Jacobi, the incumbent of the Kaiser Wilhelm Memorial Church, in the prosperous center of Berlin, also invited him. There could be little continuity in his preaching. The first sermon was at a Harvest Festival, when he preached on Psalm 63.[2] He reminded his congregation of the seven million unemployed in Germany, with even more in England and the United States. He also mentioned the millions starving in China and India, all very obvious beginnings for a Harvest Festival at that time. But his development of the sermon was challenge enough for any nominal Christian. Nearly two months later, he preached his first Advent sermon in Berlin.

November 29, 1931
Advent Sunday

*Be dressed ready for service and keep your lamps burning,
like men waiting for their master to return from a wedding
banquet, so that when he comes and knocks they can
immediately open the door for him. It will be good for those
servants whose master finds them watching when he comes.
I tell you the truth, he will dress himself to serve, will have
them recline at the table and will come and wait on them. It
will be good for those servants whose master finds them ready,
even if he comes in the second or third watch of the night. But
understand this: If the owner of the house had known at what
hour the thief was coming, he would not have let his house be
broken into. You also must be ready, because the Son of Man
will come at an hour when you do not expect him.*

Luke 12:35–40

Within this story, there is a new beatitude: "Blessed are
those servants whose master finds them watching when
he comes."

Yes, that is so—if for once, these worldly eyes look
into the face of the world of the Bible, which dissolves
into the world of Christ. But what of those to whom this
does not happen? For us today, this seems the justification for all our Christian efforts and study, the blessing

which Christ offers to us. For the others, it is our task to lift them up if there is no other way. These words of Christ are not empty of meaning. The warning follows this passage.[3] But how can Christ who loved humankind say such things about them?

But the strange fact is this: he is not speaking of a person who really fights against his ideas, nor of wrestling, striving humanity. He sees humankind already taken up within God's peace, already quite free from strife, sin, and death. Those overcome by the Spirit, Jesus sees as already under the rule of the kingdom, and they are blessed. Because Jesus sees humankind like that, we stand there where Jesus blesses us, while the unblessed, outside, are far away. Therefore we know that he is not speaking of us as we now are. But he sees us all in a quite different perspective, such as we never see ourselves. Rather as though we were covered by the eternal peace and eternal holiness of God already, as men and women who approach the state in which the new heaven and the new earth is theirs. That is seeing humanity in the perspective of God's future, in which the suffering, struggling, dying God in human history reveals himself as the First and the Last, to whom victory belongs even from the beginning. And because Christ knows of this future from his eternal wisdom, therefore he blesses humankind. We are blessed because God will come and we live already because of this coming, this overpowering of

God. We are blessed as those who wait, as those who keep awake in their waiting. Be like the one who waits for the Lord. "Blessed are those servants whose master finds them watching when he comes."

We live in a time of ideologies. Seldom, if ever, has there been a time so dominated by them; we have been disturbed and torn apart as never before. How we dress, how we eat, how we exercise—all have become ideological questions! Rarely have we become so bound by them, so doctrinaire, so intolerant as now. Naturally, we can laugh at this strange behavior, ignore it, or put it behind us . . . but it is too serious for that. It really is evident that people are not sure why they are behaving in this odd fashion. There is no doubt that something very considerable is disturbing the whole nature of our thinking. And this is the future type of person. All of us, wherever we stand ideologically, are aware that during the world events of recent years something has happened which can only be called a turning point in world history. People of today have not grown. Technology and commerce have become a law unto themselves, which threatens to destroy the human person. They raise themselves up and their demons populate the heavens, as the gods of our time. The great changes among the people drive them down and down, while no one appears strong enough to halt this inevitable fate for humankind. The artist simply reproduces what is going on around him.

Expressing this, we have shrill, toneless music and loud colors on canvas. Even religions refuse to take more than one tiny step ahead of the accepted norms. And in the knowledge of such degradation of the human person, there comes a great hope for a new kind of person, for a rebirth, for the future. Whether one sees this person as political, moral, intellectual, religious, the warrior, or the man of peace, there is basically only one concern—the new person of the future. The human person must not go under, but must triumph. The powers of this world must neither tread the person down nor enslave him. He must remain lord of the world, lord of the future. And because we wish this, we work feverishly to produce the "new man." For the clouds of the future are dark and no one knows when they will break.

And now it seems as though the Bible also has a word in support of this attempt to create a new man. It is as though the idea was already there for humanity to advance into the future. It is not the political, not the moral, not even the religious leader of which the Bible speaks, but the one who is watching and waiting, the waiting person. Of this our text speaks openly. That is the picture it paints of Jesus for all to see. It is night over the land. But there stands a house which pours light into the darkness of night. Some people ready with swords and lamps in their hands look out over the darkened land. They appear to be waiting. They are servants who await the return of their lord from the wedding, who have fought off sleep, and with joyful expectation are awake to open the door when he comes. Nobody knows the time when he will come. But they know he comes and are therefore awake in the night. How long do they wait? No one knows—perhaps they are waiting still. And now Jesus pronounces these servants "blessed," and says to the disciples: therefore be like these servants, who wait for their Lord. Make sure that you too are ready! Be waiting people. Is it not necessary for us still to say that? And we can say much more. If it is only about waiting, then surely we must all be pronounced "blessed." For what is our modern life if it is not a long wait for better times and changes? If there ever was a generation which needed to learn to wait, then it is surely ours. We wait for improved political conditions and a better economy. We wait for promotion in our employment. We wait for work. We wait for a new morality, a new religion. But in all these things, we wait anxiously. For who knows if what we are waiting for will ever come? Or if perhaps something quite different will come? And because we do not know, we must be prepared for disappointments. And for this reason, we must not lose our balance. We must stand firm.

But in our waiting there always lingers a certain amount of resignation. Our fondest hopes, all that we wish for, are weakened by an inner feeling that they may not be fulfilled. We don't want to be foolish. And it would be foolish to assume that the hopes for the future were already achieved; foolish to hold so firmly to our belief that our life would collapse if it were not to happen. Our foolish waiting would then become an agonizing waiting, an unholy selfish grabbing from one another, wanting this, that, and the other, afraid to give anything away, dreaming of the future and ignoring the benefits of the present, wanting and waiting for what eludes us. And we know quite well that that is not the kind of waiting that Jesus speaks of. Such waiting is not Advent waiting.

But when we have been through all these foolish waitings and put them behind us, something quite different waits within us. When this waiting takes possession of us, it supersedes all our foolish waiting. A longing emerges within us, which will not be silenced, a longing that all should be fulfilled amidst all the failures and against all the evidence, yet we protest its fulfillment all the stronger. This is a waiting within us for nothing less than that this world will be redeemed through and through—not by this or that political means, but by God. When God himself comes to us, then Advent truly begins to become real. When we see all our hopes and dreams shattered by questioning, by fruitless efforts and failures; when the narrowness of our existence wounds us; when suddenly we are tormented by the thought that all is lost and fallen into oblivion; and when the cry is wrenched from us: "Oh, that you would rend the heavens and come down" (Isaiah 64:1), then perhaps we can understand what the Bible means by "waiting."

When in the long night we light our lamps and peer out into the darkness, fearful lest our Lord should come soon; yes, when once hope begins to stir among us; when such signs and wonders happen, then perhaps we have not long to wait before the blessing of Jesus returns to us with power, speaking to us: "Behold! I stand at the door and knock" (Rev. 3:20, KJV). And blessed are those servants whom the Lord finds watching. And then we are really waiting.

That is truly a very different waiting from our familiar "waiting." Yes, we wait for something different, quite different—we wait for God. Waiting for God cannot be like that kind of waiting which says or thinks: "It would be wonderful if he came; but if he does not come, then we must go on living without him." We cannot wait for God so ready to resign ourselves to his not coming, so indifferent, so foolish, as we might wait for an increase in salary. No, that would be foolish, meaningless waiting if we really mean God. But if we will not be satisfied with what is offered us today as godlike words, we will go on waiting, with longing, seeking, and hoping until at last, it is God himself who comes to help and to comfort.

Then our waiting and hoping is not like a piece of wishful thinking, or a fantasy, but life itself. Then we live only because we wait for God. Then there are none of those uncertainties or reservations such as beset those who wait foolishly for foolish things. Then we step forward confidently. Much more, we see ourselves torn out of our former quiet waiting, in which we thought only of ourselves, and are changed within by an overpowering, wonderful happening, which quite without any action on our part simply happens, approaches in God's time, in God's future, in his coming to earth. That would be our future of living reality. Thus we live today under the shadow of his coming, not some dreaded disaster or some fate, but the coming of the God of justice, of love, and of peace. Not finding our own way to God into the future, but receiving the future from God. We know that we cannot go to God, but God comes to us, enfolding us in his unbelievable grace, otherwise our life is lost, and our waiting is in vain. We can only wait, watchfully wait; that means passionately waiting, totally deaf to those who would sow doubts in our mind, blind to every power that stands between us and that future which God wills for us. One thing is needful: the conviction that we shall see God, we shall hear God, we shall receive God, we shall know God, we shall serve God. In some incomprehensible way, God will—otherwise nothing, absolutely nothing else, counts.

Now then, it is really all over with our living for ourselves. God could come suddenly, while we are making our plans, and speak his true word about our life.

Frankly, any idea of planning our own lives is out. God can come suddenly, while we are planning, and speak his true word about our life. We can be fairly certain when we are dealing with other people, but no one can be sure when dealing with the living God. Then human glory is silenced. Then palaces and thrones fall. Then one stands face to face with his creator and judge, who has come to him by night. Did he find him sleeping or watching? Now, that is the question. Neither status of office or rank, nor wisdom or prudence, count for anything now. The only hope lies there, when the judgment finally comes and all eyes are upon him, waiting. All hope lies in his hands. Far above all our attempts to secure life, over all our agonizing attempts to protect our future, over all that we have done to secure our own life with our anxious busy-ness and self-torture, over all our cleverness, lies the beatitude of the waiting, watching servant and the sentence of death on the sleeping servant. The waiting servant expects everything, everything from God. Yes, he expects God himself and gives glory to him. He wants nothing for himself, all for God. Only the waiting servant is open, ready for anything. Only such can go from Advent to Christmas. Blessed are those who wait.

We cannot avoid asking the question: How can we now, in this time, make ourselves ready, so to wait that in the future we may live as we do now? How can we be sure that we shall not lose our own life in waiting only for God? The only way is to know that the God who will come in judgment has already come. It is to know that the same God who came into the midst of our history, in quiet and vulnerable stillness in Jesus Christ, is the First and the Last. God has come. Therefore all that we can do is wait and watch, praying that he will come again and again, and knowing that he will eventually come at last, no longer clothed in our history, with its suffering and death, but seen by all the world as judge and redeemer at the end of time. It is because God has come that we wait. But because his first coming into the world remains a mystery, only those who have been brought into the mystery by God himself see him, and can therefore grasp the mystery of his eternal coming again. No one is so sure of God that he need not wait for him anymore. And it is also true that no one can wait for God, who does not know that God has long been waiting for him.

And so we come back to where we started. It is not the new idea of some clever person that Jesus will stand before our eyes in reality. But it is the man of God himself, of whom Jesus speaks when he blesses the waking, waiting servant. No one becomes a man of God by his own power, but only by grace, out of the incomprehensible compassion of God, only by waiting, or perhaps not through waiting—because one can only wait because

God comes. No one can observe another to see whether he is a waiting servant. For no one can observe God coming to the other. So, let us pray earnestly that we be Christians in this hour:

"God, come in our waking hours. God, we wait for your salvation, your judgment, your love, and your peace. Jesus speak to us again, 'Behold I stand at the door and knock.' Help us now to say, 'Yes, come Lord Jesus.' Amen."[4]

December 1, 1932

Fragment of a Devotional Talk During Advent

In the third year of Cyrus king of Persia, a revelation was given to Daniel (who was called Belteshazzar). Its message was true and it concerned a great war. The understanding of the message came to him in a vision.

At that time I, Daniel, mourned for three weeks. I ate no choice food; no meat or wine touch my lips; and I used no lotions at all until the three weeks were over . . . So I was left alone, gazing at this great vision; I had no strength left, my face turned deathly pale and I was helpless. Then I heard him speaking, and as I listened to him, I fell into a deep sleep, my face to the ground . . . While he was saying this to me, I bowed

*with my face toward the ground and was speechless. Then one
who looked like a man touched my lips, and I opened my
mouth and began to speak. I said to the one standing before
me, "I am overcome with anguish because of the vision, my
lord, and I am helpless. How can I, your servant, talk with
you my lord? My strength is gone and I can hardly breathe."*

*Again the one who looked like a man touched me and gave me
strength. "Do not be afraid, O man highly esteemed," he said,
"Peace! Be strong now; be strong."*

*When he spoke to me, I was strengthened and said, "Speak,
my Lord, since you have given me strength."*

Daniel 10: 1–2, 8–9, 15–19 (full text)

I shall never forget the day when this text first deeply
impressed me. It was at a meeting of French and German
youth. We could meet together because we had common
ground in the Church and we wanted to speak frankly
and honorably about the things that lay between us.
(This was the regional youth conference of the World
Alliance, held in Westerburg, July 12–14, 1932). We
wanted seriously to place ourselves under the will of
God—in particular his command for, "Peace on earth
and goodwill towards men." And as we discussed the
demands of Christ over the world, contrasted with the
real situation in Europe and indeed the whole world, we
grew anxious. We became fearful for our message. It was

then that the words describing Daniel faced with the Word of God spoke to our condition: "So I was left alone, gazing at this great vision; I had no strength left, my face turned deathly pale and I was helpless" (v. 8). We were all too ready to shake off the responsibility of carrying this message from God, and as we were moved by this revelation, a young Frenchman read from his Bible. As he came to the words, "'Do not be afraid, O man highly esteemed,' he said, 'Peace! Be strong now; be strong.' When he spoke to me, I was strengthened" (v. 19). With one voice we all spoke, saying, "Lord, speak, for you have strengthened us."

Such a moment is strange to none of us, certainly not to any who have seriously sought to live with God. When we are disturbed by the chaos in our own personal life, when we are not ready to face it, when again and again every security fails us and there is no firm ground under our feet, when our life hangs between good intentions and shame, when it becomes inevitably clear that we are weak, when some unmanageable fate comes over us, a great sorrow or a great passion and we are horrified at the inevitable working out of this fate, when we can see only how faithless and hopeless we are caught in our errors or when friendships are finally broken, when with the best will in the world we cannot find reconciliation with the other, in short, when we take seriously the whole human chaos in which we are stuck—then it all comes over us and we say to God: Lord, I can bear no more. I can't take any more. No, I don't want any more. I am too deep in the mire. God, don't speak any more to me, for I will not hear you. God, we have nothing more to do with each other.

And then it happens that we want to hear something new and at that moment, we hear afresh: "Peace, courage." Courage, which God gives is like a mother taking hold of her child who is out of control with so many faults and failures, who is now very unhappy and begins to cry. She takes his hand and gives him a new chance: "Now, let's try that once more." Courage, courage—so God speaks to us when we are disgusted with ourselves.

And now what happened to Daniel can happen to us. His was a special occasion, which we today can understand as scarcely ever before. God says, "I will speak to you," but Daniel cannot hear. Can we? Is it not so with us, that in this unholy turmoil and helplessness, we say, "God go away!" Yes, we know it is stupid. But if you come, then it is all over. Untold anxiety, God's judgment on our people, on all we do . . . courage, courage! To what end? That we become strengthened men and women, who hear God's voice of judgment on our people and it will lead one day to a more obedient people and greater faith.[5]

Berlin

1932 – 1933

ON JANUARY 30, 1933 ADOLF HITLER was democratically elected Chancellor of Germany. The door of German history swung on its hinges and revealed a monstrous tyranny, which for twelve years rose and fell, destroying European civilization as we had known it. There were those who saw it coming and none more perceptive than the Bonhoeffer family. Towards the end of 1932, the whole atmosphere of Dietrich Bonhoeffer's sermons changed. He did not have a preaching engagement during the Advent season, but in one sermon in July 1932 on "The truth will set you free" (John 8:32), he sounded the Advent note of judgment and the whole tone of his preaching changed. There is a prophetic word in his insistence that

> the time is coming for our church when the blood of martyrs will be required. But this blood, if ever we have the courage and truth to spill it, will not be shining and pure like that of the first martyrs. Our own guilt lies heavy upon our blood: the guilt of the unprofitable servant, who was cast out into the darkness.[1]

In the last sermons of this Berlin period, the word "revolution" is often used, not metaphorically, but literally. And there are references also to the "revolutionary" elements in the Christian message.

The few sermons preached in the early months of 1933 are outspoken in their warning of times to come as the

Nazis rose to power. For these reasons, I have included in this section sermons that stress the urgent Advent demands upon the church to rise to the hour of danger, signaled by the events of January 30.

July 24, 1932 (preached at the closing of the university semester)

John 8:32

The Truth Will Set You Free

That is perhaps the most revolutionary phrase in the whole of the New Testament. It is not directed to the mass of people as a whole, but only to the few genuine revolutionaries. It is therefore a quite exclusive phrase. For the general public it remains a mystery—or it becomes a soundbite, which is the most dangerous of all. Used as a soundbite, it just takes the edge off the real revolution.

Who is then this exclusive group of people whom Jesus addresses? Is it the powerful politicians or the professional revolutionaries and their followers? Is it the champions of freedom among all kinds of people? Is it those who battle for knowledge and progress? Where do we find this group and what are they like, the people for whom this phrase is valid? I will describe a situation which I think all of us have at some time experienced. A group of grown-up people have assembled. In the course of their discussion, a subject arises which cannot be avoided, but which is extraordinarily painful for some of the group. It leads to a very unpleasant argument, full of falsehood and anger. A child happens to be there, who of course does not grasp the full situation, but knows something which all the others know, but are afraid to mention. The child is surprised that the others do not seem to know what he knows, and blurts it out. An embarrassed silence goes around the group. The child looks around with surprise. They stare at the child in confusion. The child laughs and is happy that he has said the right thing. Yet something irreparable has happened. The words full of falsehood and anger have been cut off at a stroke. A piercing light has fallen upon the lies and angry words, quite suddenly. They are completely exposed. They fall helpless in confusion before this light. What has happened is none other than that through this wonder child, the truth has come to light among the grown-ups. The word of the child has unmasked the hypocrisy of the adults, in their own attitudes and with one another. What has happened here is quite revolutionary. And by whom has this happened? By the wonderful laughing, fearless child, who described the thing which bothered them. Only the child was free.

And another illustration: imagine the court of a prince, where knights, singers, and poets surround their prince with flattery and lies. But there is one man who by his clothing does not appear to belong there. He is out of place. His dress is comic. They treat him as one who doesn't count. He appears to be an exception to the usual guests at court. And yet, they need this exception. He does not belong, but he is indispensable to the court. He is the fool, the jester. He was the only one who dared to tell the truth about each of them and they must all listen to him. He was quite unimportant, but they could not dispense with him. In much the same manner are we related to the truth, in that he was the only free man at court.

And now the third illustration. Those who have rightly understood the first two parables will not be surprised at whom I have chosen for the third—the man who has been flogged and humiliated, crowned in jest with thorns, he who is himself the king of truth now stands before his judge. Pilate asks the clever, but so far as this world is concerned, quite hopeless question: What is truth? He directs this question to the one who has himself said, I am the truth! And now, because he is the truth, gives Pilate his question back to him in silence: Who are you, Pilate, when faced with the truth, with me? What happens now is none other than that the truth itself will be crucified and that Pilate will be judged by crucified truth. You do not ask about truth, truth asks about you. The crucified king of truth, to whom we pray, that is the third image that we look upon when we hear the New Testament talk about truth. The child, the fool, the crucified—a strange selection of people to be called saviors of humankind, or revolutionaries. But now we know even more clearly to whom we should turn our gaze when we hear the words: "The Truth will set you free."

In human life the truth is strange, unusual, exceptional. It is as when something quite unexpected and powerful breaks into our life, or where somewhere the truth is spoken. It can happen that when our ears are full of the sound of the band that the full truth may be spoken. But the truth on the program is no longer real truth. Real truth is distinguished from mere words, however correct they may be, by what happens of importance—that people are released by it, set free. Those who until then have lived with lies, without freedom and full of anxiety, are given freedom. And it is now the crystal-clear word of the Bible that those who are enslaved by lies are set free by the truth that comes only from God. It is all too easy today for us to talk about freedom, and by so speaking, to rouse the emotions of us Germans about the growth of our suffering and to forget everything else. It may be that there are many in Germany today, as once there were among the Hebrews enslaved in Egypt, who could dream of nothing else than freedom. Great dreams of liberty and taking hold of it. But then comes the awakening when the vision fades. Yes, it is easy to talk of freedom in Germany today. But it is much more difficult to talk of freedom in the way that the Bible talks of it. The truth will make us free, but that truth is always untimely. Our actions, our strength, our courage, our race, our morality—in short, we shall make ourselves free. We can understand why it is popular. But what place does this down-to-earth word, "truth" play in all this? The word "truth" has become unpopular. We suspect this word has something against us. It has a sharp edge. Today, one cannot bear to be unpopular; when great words are in every mouth, in religious, political, and secular affairs, how can one put the sobering question: Yes, is all this true? No one would listen. It sounds so critical, so destructive, so intolerant, so cold, so negative. We all live in constant, insurmountable fear of the truth, even if we don't know it. Yes, and even if we do, we think that we are ourselves called upon to bring truth into the world. We are always afraid that someone will come along, who sees more deeply than we do and with his critical insights will look at our words and take them to pieces. And from greater fear, we speak more loudly and emphatically as though we knew the truth. We are all afraid of the truth. And this fear is basically our anxiety in the presence of God. God is the truth and no other. And before him we fear that he will stand us in the light of truth, and expose all our lies. The truth is a power, a force, which is held over us and can destroy us at any moment. It is not the high heaven of concepts and ideas, but the sword of God, the threatened lightning which destroys and exposes us. The truth is the living God himself and his word which comes to us.

In the presence of this truth, we die; but because we are clever, we do not see the truth and, therefore, will not die. To do this we have to learn ever more sophisticated, more profound, well thought out lies. Therefore we entrench ourselves so deeply into these lies that we no longer know that they are lies. We believe our lies to be the truth. And that is where we are. And because we are in such a state, all that I have been saying is taken for exaggeration and people do not believe it is true.

Of course, you would agree that there are such matters as political lies and white lies, which are commonly accepted lies in social life. These lies by which we live in commerce or polite society have such a strong hold on us. What we cannot imagine is that an event should occur in which all the covering up and careful hiding falls away, so that we now stand with the truth revealed. We have no idea until it happens, how deeply our whole being would be exposed. We know only one thing—that if this happened, the life we now live would be impossible. We can only live this kind of life so long as we are not in the full light of day, but in the obscurity of the night. But surely what is happening to us is not like the last judgment. Or is it?

If you protest that what I have said is not true, that there are so many lies around you and in you, then you will soon become inveterate liars and your protest goes on until something quite unexpected happens. Eventually, we encounter God himself as the truth and he himself does what we cannot do: he places us directly in front of himself, in the truth, where we stand revealed as inveterate liars in our whole being. Here there are no excuses, no mercy. Here we are brought before the Judge. Here we can no longer talk of this or that acceptable lie, but we ourselves are accused.

And then something happens against which we have no power—now the truth comes. It encounters us in an unexpected form, not with trailing clouds of glory and dazzling clarity, but as the crucified truth, as the crucified Christ. And the truth speaks to us. It says to us, "Who has crucified me, the truth?" And in the same moment it answers itself, "See what you have done. You have hated the truth of God. You have crucified it. And you have set up your own truth. You believed you knew the truth, you possessed it, you thought to make men happy with your truth and you have thereby made yourself into God. You have robbed God of his truth and proclaimed your own truth instead—but you have thereby ruined yourself by playing God and with that comes destruction. You have crucified truth."

And if we should find this mystery too difficult for us to understand, listen to what the truth says more clearly: You are living as though you were alone in the world. You have thought to find within yourself the source of truth, which can only be found in God. For that reason you hate the other person who does the same. You found in yourself the center of the world and this is the source of the lie. You saw your brothers as part of your personal kingdom, lording it over them and not seeing that you and they live by the truth of God. You tear yourself out of communion with God and your brother and think you can live alone. You hate God and your brother because they deny your truth. That was the lie and you are therefore liars through and through. Your wish to be alone, self-sufficient, and your hatred of others—that is the lie. For that reason you crucified God's truth. You thought you would become free if you tore away and hated the truth. But you have become a slave, a slave of your hatred and a slave of your lies. The way to truth and freedom is closed to you. It leads only to the cross, and to death. That is what the truth says to us. Its last word to us with our so called truth is quite simply—death! For it is the crucified truth itself which speaks to us the living word. Who knows when? Today? Tomorrow? At the last judgment?

Something very special is indicated here. Our lies are lies against God. They arm themselves against the reality and the truth of God, against his communion and grace, and against his love. Our lies hate the love of God, because they imagine that they have no need of it. The substance of our lies is hate, because the substance of the truth of God is grace and love. One thing becomes clear—truth and lies are not what one says, but what one does. The totality of how one lives. Whoever lives in the lie, lives on hate. That means such people live in chains of their own making. They are bound in fetters. They are slaves to themselves. To recognize this is the beginning of recognizing the truth, which comes alone from God. Whoever is aware of being the slave of lies, anxiety, and hate has been placed in the truth by God. Such people now see that all their supposed freedom was only slavery and all their supposed truth was lies. And whoever hears this, experiences an inexpressible yearning to be freed from their bondage: "Lord make me free from myself." From that new encounter comes to him the words: The truth will make you free.

It is not something that we have to do, not our courage, our church, our people, our truth; but God's truth alone that makes us free. Why? Because to become free does not mean becoming great in the world, not becoming free from your brother, nor even free from God, but to become free from oneself, one's lie. It means to become free from thinking only of myself, from being the center of my world, from hate, by which I despise God's creation. It means to be free to be for the other: the person for others. Only God's truth can enable me to see the other as he really is. It tears out the twisted image that I have of the other within me and shows him to me in a new light. And insofar as God's truth does that, it bestows upon me the action, the love, the grace of God. It destroys our lies and creates the truth. It destroys hatred and creates love. God's truth is God's love and God's love makes us free from ourselves for others. To be free means nothing less than to be in love. And to be in love means nothing less than being in the truth of God. The man who loves because he has been made free by God is the most revolutionary man on earth. He challenges all values. He is the explosive material of human society. He is a dangerous man. For he recognizes that the human race is in the depths of falsehood. And he is always ready to let the light of truth fall upon his darkness; and he will do this because of his love. But this disturbance, which such people bring, calls forth hatred from the world. And therefore this knight of truth and love is not the hero that men long for or honor, not one who is without enemies; but one whom they would do away with, outlaw, and indeed kill. The way of God's truth leads to the cross. From now on, we know that all truth which is true before God must face the cross. The church that follows Christ must go with him to the cross. Because of its truth and freedom it will be hated by the world. It is also true that a people cannot find truth and freedom unless it stands under the law of God's truth. A people (*Volk*) remains in lies and in slavery until it receives and wants to receive truth and freedom from God alone; until it knows that truth and freedom will lead it into love; yes, until it knows that the way of love leads to the cross. If a people would really know this, then it would become the only people who could rightly be called a free people, the only people which does not become a slave to itself, but the slave of the truth of God and therefore free.

We all, each one individually for himself or herself, and as a people, feel the pressing weight of our chains. O God, protect us, that we are not entranced by the deceitful image of freedom and the temptation to remain in our lies. Give to us that freedom which throws us upon Thee and Thy grace. Lord, with thy truth, make us, as our Lord Jesus Christ is, truly free. Lord we wait upon Thy truth.

July 23, 1933

(the last sermon in Berlin)

Hitler had ordered church elections, which meant an electoral conflict between the "German Christians" and the Young Reformation Movement which opposed them. Bonhoeffer was involved in the preparation of election leaflets, which the Gestapo confiscated before they could be used. The election was rigged, with Hitler making a personal appeal on radio for support of the "German Christians." The result was 70 percent for the German Christians. Bonhoeffer preached his last sermon in Berlin on that day, July 23, 1933 in Trinity Church.

The Search for the Church of Peter

When Jesus came to the region of Caesarea Philippi, he asked his disciples, "Who do people say the Son of Man is?" They replied, "Some say John the Baptist; others say Elijah; and still others, Jeremiah or one of the prophets." "But what about you" he asked, "Who do you say I am?" Simon Peter answered, "You are the Christ, the Son of the living God." Jesus replied, "Blessed are you, Simon son of Jonah, for this was not revealed to you by man, but by my Father in heaven. And I tell you that you are Peter, and on this rock I will build my church, and the gates of Hades will not overcome it."

Matthew 16:13–18

If it were left to us, we would rather avoid the decisions which are forced upon us this day; if it were left to us, we would rather not be caught up in this struggle in the Church, which tears it apart; if it were left to us, we would rather not insist upon the rightness of our cause. We would willingly avoid the terrible danger of exalting ourselves over others. If it were left to us, we would rather retire today than tomorrow into the quietness of the countryside, and leave the strife and the pride others. But, in fact, it is not—thank God!—left to us. God has planned otherwise. We are called upon to make a decision from which we cannot escape. We must be content, wherever we are, to face the accusation of being self-righteous, of acting and speaking as though we were proud and superior to others. Nothing is made easy for us. We are confronted with a decision and we are divided. For this reason, we must be honest with ourselves and not disguise the true meaning of the church elections today.

Amidst the creaking and straining of the very foundations of its structure, amidst the cracks and destruction, we hear everywhere the promise of an everlasting church; a church against which the powers of hell shall not prevail. A church which Christ has built upon a rock, and which he continues to build throughout all time.

Where is this church? Where do we find it? Where do we hear its voice? Come! All you who in earnest ask such questions, all you who are abandoned and are left alone, all you who have lost the church. We will go once again back to the Holy Scriptures. Together, we will go in search of the everlasting church. Who hath ears to hear, let him hear. Jesus went out to a desert place, alone with his disciples, on the very edge of the pagan world. Here he is alone with them. And here in this place, he promises his legacy of an everlasting church. It was not in the presence of the multitude, not in the climax of his miracles, but far from the theologically-sound scribes, from the Pharisees, and from the masses, who will cry "Hosanna" on Palm Sunday and "crucify" on Good Friday.

It was not where one might have expected the announcement; but it was this lonely place that he spoke to the disciples of the mystery and the future of his church. It was quite clear that this church would not be built upon the learning of the scribes, the holiness of the priests, nor upon the fickle crowds, but upon that small group of disciples that followed him. It was obvious that he did not consider Jerusalem, the city of the temple and the heart of the nation, as the proper place to build it; but into a lonely place he goes to make his proclamation, where he could not hope to get publicity. Finally, he had not chosen some great feast day of his religion to speak of his church, but he made this promise of his church just before the announcement of his coming death. So, what must be meant here is the church of the small group, the church in the wilderness, the church facing death.

Jesus himself poses the decisive question for which the disciples had long waited: First, "Who do the people say the Son of Man is?" The answer comes simply, "Some say you are John the Baptist, some that you are Elijah, some say you are Jeremiah, or one of the prophets." One could multiply these opinions, endlessly—some say a great man, some say of you, an idealist, some say you are a religious genius, others say you are a hero, a powerful leader. Opinions, all of them different views, but Christ will not build his church upon opinions. Therefore, he poses the really decisive question: "And who do you say that I am?" In this unavoidable encounter with Christ, there is no "perhaps" or "some say," no longer an opinion, but only silence or the one answer, which Peter gives: "Thou art the Christ, the Son of the living God." Here in the midst of the storm of human opinions, something quite new appears. Here, God is named. Here the eternal is expressed, here the mystery is made known. Here there are no longer human opinions, but precisely the opposite. Here is divine revelation and confession of faith. "Blessed are you, Simon son of Jonah, for this was not revealed to you by man, but by my Father in heaven . . . you are Peter, and on this rock I will build my church." How does Peter differ from the others? Is he of such heroic nature that he tops the rest? He is not. Has he such an unheard of strength of character? He has not. Is he unshakably faithful? He is not. Peter is nothing, absolutely nothing more than a man who believes; a man whom Christ has met on the way and recognized, and who now confesses his faith. And Christ calls this confessing Peter the rock, on which he will build his church.

Peter's church—that means the church built on the rock, the church of those confessing Christ, the Confessing Church—not the church of opinions and ideas, but the church of revelation. Not the church which becomes what one says or what "the people say," but the church in which the confession of Peter is said again and again and passed on; the church which is concerned only with singing, praying, preaching, doing, and reaching out with the confession, always and only; the church which remains only so long as it has the rock beneath it, and as soon as it builds its house upon the sand it is blasted by the wind. And this will happen whatever alternative foundation it seeks, or rests upon for even a moment.

But Peter's church—that is not something which one could say with untroubled pride. Peter, the confessing, believing disciple; who, on the same night that Judas betrayed his master, denied that he ever knew him. In that same night, standing by the fire, he was ashamed as Christ stood before the High Priest. He is the follower of little faith who sinks in the water on the lake. He is the disciple to whom Jesus spoke those terrible words: "Out of my sight Satan!" He is the one who, again and again, was weak, denying, and failing, a weakling of little courage, easily swayed by those he was with. Peter's church, that is the church to which these weaklings belong. The church which again and again betrays and fails, the unfaithful, the people of little faith, a frightened church, which is constantly departing from its mission in the world and the reason for its existence. Peter's church, that is the church of those who are ashamed of their Lord, when they should instead be standing up for him.

But Peter's church is now also that of whom it is said, "He went out and wept bitterly." Of Judas, who also betrayed the Lord, it is said, he went out and hanged himself. That is the difference. Peter went out and wept bitterly; Peter's church which can still weep. "By the rivers of Babylon we sat and wept when we remembered Zion" (Psalm 137:1). That is the church. For what is weeping other than to have found the way back? To be back home? To be like the prodigal son, who falls on his knees before his father, weeping? Peter's church is the church with divine sadness which leads to rejoicing.

Surely a weak foundation is it not? But made of rock! For this Peter, this broken reed, is called by God, imprisoned by God, formed by God: "You are Peter." We are all Peter. Not only the Pope, as the Catholics would have it. Not this one or that one, but all of us, we who live simply by confessing Christ, we who are fearful, faithless, or of little faith, and yet formed by God.

But it is not we who should build, but he who will build. No human hand builds the church, but Christ alone. Whoever thinks he can build the church is already destroying it. For what he is building is a temple for idols, without knowing or wishing it.

We shall confess—he shall build. We shall preach— he shall build. We shall pray to him—he shall build. We do not know his plan. We do not see whether he builds or tears down. It may be that the times, which by human standards are times of collapse, are for him the times of great building. It may be that the times, which by human standards are times of great success, are for him times to tear down. It is a great comfort that Christ gives to his church: confess, preach, and bear witness to me. I alone will build as it pleases me. Don't give me orders. Do your job—then you have done enough. You are all right. Don't seek out reasons and opinions. Don't keep judging. Don't keep checking again and again to see if you are secure. Church, remain a church! But, you, church— confess, confess, confess! You have only one Lord— Christ alone. By his grace alone you live. Christ builds.

And the power of hell shall not overcome you. Death is the legacy of all who live. Here it finds its end. On the hard foundations of the valley of death, the church is built, the church which confesses Christ as its life. It has eternal life precisely where death grasps at it. And it grasps at it because it has eternal life. The confessing church is the everlasting church, because Christ protects it. Its eternal nature is not visible in this world. It is persecuted by the world. The waves go high over it and sometimes it appears to sink and be lost. But the victory lies with the church, because Christ the Lord is with it and he has conquered death. "Do not ask if the victory is yours, but believe in the victory and it is already yours."

The words of our text are inscribed around the dome of the great Church of St. Peter in Rome, the Pope's church. This church is proud of its eternal nature, its visible victory over the world through the centuries. Our heart neither envies nor seeks such glory, but rather refuses it. But there is a glory, which by any standards, is far greater than this, of which we are sure. Whether the numbers are great or small, whether the members are lowly or high, whether they are weak or strong, if they confess Christ, the victory is theirs through all eternity: "Do not be afraid, little flock, for your Father has been pleased to give you the kingdom" (Luke 12:32). "For where two or three come together in my name, there am I with them" (Matthew 18:20). The city of God remaineth!

London

1933 – 1935

AFTER THE CHURCH ELECTIONS OF JULY 23, 1933, the victory of the German Christians gave them control of the National Church. The opposition attempted to reduce the harmful effects, particularly the exclusion of those members and pastors of Jewish origin from the National Church. In this Bonhoeffer went far beyond his colleagues and felt separated from those he most respected. He expressed his doubts in a letter to Karl Barth when he had an invitation to go to London to minister to two German-speaking congregations:

> I feel that in some way I don't understand, I find myself in radical opposition to all my friends; I became increasingly isolated with my views of things ... All this has frightened me and shaken my confidence so that I began to fear that dogmatism might be leading me astray ... and so I thought it was about time to go into the wilderness for a spell ... It seems to me at the moment it is more dangerous for me to make a gesture than to retreat into silence.[1]

On October 16, 1933, Bonhoeffer left for London. Two days earlier, Hitler had announced that Germany had left the League of Nations, because of the rejection of his demand for "equality of status." Even the opposition welcomed this. In the name of the Pastors' Emergency League (which had succeeded the Young Reformation Movement), Martin Niemöller sent a telegram to the Führer "expressing gratitude and swearing loyal allegiance." Bonhoeffer did not share this view, but is reported as saying, "This has brought the danger of war very much closer."

"The Wilderness"

London was anything but "the wilderness" he sought! The idea of quiet pastoral work, preaching, teaching, and caring for the members of two congregations who were removed from the conflicts in Germany, was soon dispelled. He was in daily communication with Berlin on the telephone. The eighteen months he spent in London were dominated by the church struggle. George Bell, Bishop of Chichester, involved him further in the ecumenical movement and depended upon him for information about the church struggle. But he did not neglect his parishes, nor sideline his preaching. He preached every Sunday and once a month he preached in English! In his eighteen months he must have preached between seventy and eighty sermons. Only sixteen of these have survived in manuscript form. The involvement in the church struggle, both directly with Berlin and at ecumenical conferences, his active work among pastors of other German congregations in England, and much else inevitably came into his sermons. But on the whole, he kept his eye on the congregations he was serving and spoke to them of their need and proclaimed the gospel of salvation. The German Christians had talked of building a new church in a new state. He persistently repeated, "Christ builds, and Christ alone." While he was in London, the opposition organized itself as the Confessing Church (a phrase he had used in his last sermon in Berlin) on the basis of a Confession, written and accepted in Barmen in 1934. Before leaving Berlin, his attempts to write that Confession with his colleagues led to disappointment, because they watered down the strong condemnations of the treatment of the Jews. But he supported the Confessing Church and as a result was almost removed from his charge. After much controversy, the church retained him with renewed affection, until he was recalled to Germany to lead a Preachers Seminary of the Confessing Church.

Pastor Bonhoeffer in London

As in Barcelona, Bonhoeffer attempted to introduce all kinds of activities in his churches: a children's Sunday school, youth clubs, and performances of nativity and passion plays. Although he approved of collections for the Winter Aid Fund (Goebbels had set this up for all the churches in Germany and overseas), he insisted that there should also be collections for German refugees in England. Bethge points out that his congregations found him rather too demanding. Of his sermons, he says:

> His parishioners found the severe standards of his sermons particularly hard to accept. They were accustomed to the mild, folksy, pious sermons of his predecessor. Bonhoeffer's sermons, by comparison, seemed too oppressive and emphatic. Indeed, some responded by staying away.[2]

The Sermons (Advent)

Among the surviving sermon manuscripts, there are two during Advent 1933, but none for the following Advent. In fact, the last surviving sermon is from November 4, 1934. That sermon on Reformation Sunday is the last of four sermons on 1 Corinthians 13, carefully nurturing the spirituality of his people. But that is not Advent preaching!

The two Advent sermons included here, therefore, are from the early part of his ministry in London. The first sermon in his new pastorate was on October 22, 1933, Trinity Sunday, on the theme "Messenger of Reconciliation" (2 Corinthians 5:20).

December 3, 1933
Advent Sunday—

How a Prisoner Waits
for His Release!

*When these things begin to take place, stand up and lift up
your heads, because your redemption is drawing near.*

Luke 21:28

You all know what a mining disaster is. In these last few
weeks, we must all have read again and again in our
newspapers about the disaster in Wales. In the coalmines
in Wales there are men who daily must go down into the
depths of the earth to do their work, despite the dangers
which hang over them. They know that one day an
underground explosion might destroy one of the gal-
leries—and now it has. They are trapped deep in the
earth, dark as night, cut off, alone. Their fate is sealed.
What all their life they have dreaded has come to these
brave miners. Calling out is no help. However hard they
bang against the wall, nothing is accomplished. All their
strength is unavailing: the more a man recognizes his
helplessness, the more he rages against it . . . but all is
still. He knows that up there, the people are moving
about, the women and children are crying—but the way

to them is blocked. There is no hope. Of course, they know that there are men up there working feverishly to reach them and their comrades.

There they are digging with all their energy, breaking through the stone and moving the rubble. Perhaps here or there one more may be found and rescued. But here in the deepest depths of the lowest shaft, there is no hope. There remains only agony and waiting for death. And what if then, a light sound is heard, like a knocking, a hammer blow, a breaking of stone! And if suddenly, a voice can be heard from far away, calling, calling from nowhere, calling in the dark, these sounds and activities come a little louder and nearer, until a hard blow comes quite near. It all stops suddenly and then a friendly voice of a man is heard, a comrade, shouting out an imprisoned man's name, saying, "Where are you?" And adds, "Help is coming," then the helpless man stands up, his heart leaps from its tension and waiting to muster all his remaining energy to cry aloud, "Here I am!" and adds, "Come through to me and help me." He confesses his weakness as he says, "I cannot come through. I cannot help myself. But I wait, I wait and will hold on until you come. Only, come quickly." Now, he listens with agonizing attention as blow after blow comes nearer. Seconds seem like hours. He sees nothing, nothing at all, but he hears the voice of the helper. Then comes a last wild, smashing blow of the hammer to his ear, and the rescuer is almost there. One strike more and he is free. Now, you are wondering why I am talking about all this on Advent Sunday. It is really about Advent that I am speaking. These events are precisely what happens in the drawing near of God to humankind, the coming of deliverance, the arrival of Christ. "Stand up and lift up your heads, because your redemption is drawing near." To whom is this addressed? Whom does this word really interest? Who is most affected by this announcement?

Think of a prison. For long years, the prisoners have born the shame and punishment of their imprisonment. Hard forced labor has plagued them, until life itself has become a burden. Again and again, they have tried one way or another to escape, but they were caught and brought back to even harsher conditions than they had before. Even if some escape, the others suffer. With sighs and tears these others lament their loss and hate their chains. And now suppose that a message came to the prison: "Within a short time, you will all be free. Your chains will fall off. Your tormentors will be bound and you will be delivered." Can you not hear the prisoners with one voice crying out with all their heart: "Yes. Deliverer, come!"

Think of a hospital where a patient lies, suffering from an incurable disease, in agony with indescribable pain, dying slowly, and slowly longing for the peace of death to end this plague. And now, one day, the doctor comes to the patient and says with confidence: "Today, you will be released. Your terminal illness will be healed. Lift up your head and be delivered from your pain."

And now, think of those people who are not in prison, not terminally ill, but who are in deep depression. Think of those who have a secret, about whom we spoke on Penitence Sunday (*Busstag*) two weeks ago. Think of those who live guilty with unforgiven sins and who have lost the feeling for life, and because of it all happiness and joy has gone. Think about ourselves. We usually live a Christian and obedient life, but from time to time betray it. Think of the son who cannot look his father in the face, or the man who cannot look his wife in the face. Think of the limitless destruction and hopelessness that arises out of all these situations—and then let us again hear: "Stand up and lift up your heads, because your redemption is drawing near." You will become free from all this. The sorrow and anguish of your soul will come to an end. Deliverance is near. Just as a father says to his son: Look up, don't turn your eyes to the ground, look at me. I am your father . . . that is what the words in the Gospel mean, "Look up, lift up your head, because your deliverance is drawing near." And so, who is really addressed by this text? Those who know that they are not free, that they are enslaved and bound, that a power controls them to which they must pay service; those who are like people buried alive, like those prisoners, who look constantly for freedom, real deliverance; people who long to be delivered. But these words are not directed to those who are already quite content with their condition, who have no idea that they are imprisoned; those who have come to terms with their unfree condition, even for practical purposes; those who are totally indifferent and unimpressed when they hear the call, "Your deliverance is drawing nigh." Not for the satisfied and contented, but for those who hunger and thirst, these words are directed—this Advent call! It is for such that he knocks, loud and clear. And we hear him, like the trapped miner who hears every movement of the rescuers and follows every blow as it comes nearer, until the breakthrough. Can you imagine that he would not, from the moment he heard the first sound, listen intensively, eagerly anticipating his release? And now, do we say that the Advent call is different from that: your deliverance, the deliverance of all of you, is drawing near. There is a knock at the door. Don't you hear it? It will guide you through all the rubble, the stoniness of your heart. That doesn't happen quickly, but it comes. Christ breaks his way through to you, to your heart. Hearts that become hard, he softens in obedience to him. Again, he calls us even in these weeks of waiting, weeks of waiting for Christmas and he says he is coming. He is coming to rescue us from the prisons of our existence, from anxieties, from guilt, and from loneliness.

Do you want to be delivered? That is the only really important and decisive question which Advent poses for us. Does there burn within us some lingering longing to know what deliverance really means?

If not, what would Advent then mean to us? A bit of sentimentality. A little lifting of the spirit within us? A little kinder mood? But, if there is something in this word Advent which we have not yet known, that strangely warms our heart; if we suspect that it could, once more, once more, mean a turning point in our life, a turning to God, to Christ—why then are we not simply obedient, listening and hearing in our ears the clear call: Your deliverance draws nigh! Wait, just one moment, wait, the knocking will grow louder, hour by hour, day by day, becoming ever more clear. And when Christmas comes and we are ready, God comes to us, to you and to me. Christ the Savior is here!

Perhaps you say: all this has been said in the church so many times before but it has never happened! Why is it that nothing has happened? Because we did not want it to. Because we would neither listen, nor believe. Because we said: It could be that here or there, perhaps one or another trapped person was rescued, but as for us, we are too deep down, so far away from these things, that the deliverer will not get through. We are not pious people. We are not particularly religious. It's all very well, but don't give us all this once again. We are lost with all this talk. We know it all. Who among us has not been taught it? If what you say were really simple, without all these words and excuses, we might eventually give our time, we might eventually begin to pray. Then this Advent would not pass us by unmoved. Don't deceive yourselves, the Savior comes near whether we know it or not. And the question is only: Shall we let this deliverance come to us or shall we refuse it? Shall we join with this movement which comes from heaven to earth or shall we oppose it? Christmas will come in this way, whether we are part of this movement or not.

Our text makes two powerful demands clear, helping us to understand the true nature of the Advent event. It is not the miserable, weak, anxious Advent of popular "Christian" celebration, which we are so often contented with and which Christ deplores. The two demands are clear: "Look up. Raise your head." Advent makes people whole: new people. We can also become new people in Advent. Stand up, look up, your view is too much down towards the earth, fixed upon the superficial changes and happenings of this earth. Look up, you who have turned away disappointed from heaven, see this Advent word. Look up, you whose eyes are heavy with tears and who mourn that the earth has snatched everything from you. Look up, you who are so heavy laden with guilt that you feel you cannot look up. Look up, your salvation draws near. When you look up, things look quite different from what you have seen day by day, more real, far greater, and more powerful. If only it were true. Be patient. Wait for a little while longer. Wait and something quite new will come over you. God will come. Jesus comes and takes up his abode with you and you become a redeemed people. Look up, stand, and watch. Keep your eyes open, waiting for the approaching deliverance. Lift up your heads—you army of men and women, bowed down with sorrow, demoralized, without hope, you defeated army of drooping heads. The battle is not yet lost. Lift up your heads. Yours is the victory. Take courage. Have no fear, no anxiety, no sorrow. Courage! Make the victory sure. Be strong, be able. Here there is no reason to droop your head, no more doubts, no uncertainty of the way. Freedom, salvation, and deliverance come. Look up; raise your heads. Be fearless and strong! Because Christ comes.

And now we ask once more: Do we now hear the knock and go forward, as though something springs up within us urging us to become free? Do we encounter Christ? Are we to believe that this is not just pious talk, but that something really happens? That the human soul, shattered and torn apart, will be put right and become whole? What, when God draws near to earth with clouds of glory, and sinful humans tremble with fear, there will be hope and joy? That God himself draws near to human souls and enters into them? Can the trapped miners concern themselves with anything but the hammers and the blows of the rescuers? Can and should there be anything else more important for us than the hammers and blows of Jesus Christ coming into our lives? And in view of all that is happening, can we do anything other than prick up our ears and listen, with fear and trembling, stretching out for him? This is at work in us. We have nothing to add to it, no action, but let him come as he will. In mid-winter, Luther had once preached on this text of ours, as Advent came, calling out: "The summer is near. The trees burgeon. It is springtime." Whoever has ears to hear, let him hear.[3]

December 17, 1933

Third Sunday in Advent— My Soul Praises the Lord

And Mary said: "My soul glorifies the Lord and my spirit rejoices in God my Savior, for he has been mindful of the humble state of his servant. From now on all generations will call me blessed, for the Mighty One has done great things for me—holy is his name. His mercy extends to those who fear him, from generation to generation. He has performed mighty deeds with his arm; he has scattered those who are proud in their inmost thoughts. He has brought down the rulers from their thrones but has lifted up the humble. He has filled the hungry with good things, but has sent the rich away empty.

He has helped his servant Israel, remembering to be merciful to Abraham and his descendants forever, even as he said to our fathers."

Luke 1:46–55

This song of Mary's is the oldest Advent hymn. It is the most passionate, most vehement, one might almost say, most revolutionary Advent hymn ever sung. It is not the gentle, sweet, dreamy Mary that we so often see portrayed in pictures, but the passionate, powerful, proud, enthusiastic Mary, who speaks here. None of the sweet, sugary, or childish tones that we find so often in our Christmas hymns, but a hard, strong, uncompromising song of bringing down rulers from their thrones and humbling the lords of this world, of God's power and of the powerlessness of men. These are the tones of the prophetic women of the Old Testament: Deborah, Judith, Miriam, coming alive in the mouth of Mary.

Mary, filled with the Spirit and prepared. Mary, the obedient handmaid, humbly accepting what is to happen to her, what the Spirit asks of her, to do with her as the Spirit will, speaks now by the Spirit of the coming of God into the world, of the Advent of Jesus Christ. She knows better than anyone what it means to wait for Christ. He is nearer to her than to anyone else. She awaits him as his mother. She knows about the mystery of his coming, of the Spirit who came to her, of the Almighty God who works his wonders. She experiences in her own body that God does wonderful things with the children of men, that his ways are not our ways, that he cannot be predicted by men, or circumscribed by their reasons and ideas, but that his way is beyond all understanding or explanations, both free and of his own will.

Where our reason is offended, where our nature rebels, where our piety creeps anxiously away, there, precisely there, God loves to be. There, he confuses the understanding of the clever. There he offends our nature, our piety. There he will dwell and no one can deny him. And now, only the humble can believe him, and rejoice that God is so free and so wonderful, that he works miracles when the children of men despair. He has made the lowly and humble to be lifted up. That is the wonder of wonders, that God loves the lowly: "God has been mindful of the humble state of his servant."

God in the "humble state"—that is the revolutionary, the passionate word of Advent. First, Mary herself, the wife of a carpenter. We may say, the poor working man's wife, unnoticed by men—but now, insignificant and in her humble state as we might see it, she is significant to God and appointed to be the mother of the Savior of the world. Not because of some remarkable human trait in her, not because of some great piety, not because of her modesty, not because of any particular virtue in her, but apart from any of these characteristics, only because

God's gracious will is to love the humble and lowly, the insignificant. He chose to make them great. Mary, living in the faith of the Old Testament and hoping for her redeemer, this humble working man's wife becomes the mother of God. Christ the son of a poor working man's wife in the East End of London! Christ in the manger . . . God is not ashamed to be with those of humble state. He goes into the midst of it all, chooses one person to be his instrument, and does his miracle there, where one least expects it. He loves the lost, the forgotten, the insignificant, the outcasts, the weak, and the broken. Where men say, "lost," he says "found;" where men say, "condemned," he says "redeemed;" where men say "no," he says "yes." Where men look with indifference or superiority, he looks with burning love, such as nowhere else is to be found. Where men say, "contemptible!," God cries, "blessed." When we reach a point in our lives at which we are not only ashamed of ourselves, but believe God is ashamed of us too, when we feel so far from God, more than we have ever felt in our lives, then and precisely then, God is nearer to us than he has ever been. It is then that he breaks into our lives. It is then that he lets us know that that feeling of despair is taken away from us, so that we may grasp the wonder of his love, his nearness to us, and his grace. "From now on all generations will call me blessed," says Mary. What does that mean? Mary, a maid of "humble state," called "blessed?" It can

be no other than the miracle of God that he has aston-
ishingly performed on her; God has been "mindful of the
humble state" of Mary and raised her up; God, coming
into the world, seeks out, not the high and mighty, but
the lowly; that we might see the glory and the mighty
power of God making the down and out great. To call
Mary "blessed" does not mean to build her an altar; but
with her to pray to God, who is mindful of the lowly and
chooses them, who has done great things—holy is his
name. To call Mary blessed is to know with her that
God's "mercy extends to those who fear him," those who
watch and consider his astonishing ways, who let his
Spirit blow where it will, those who are obedient to him
and with Mary, humbly say, "May it be to me as you
have said."

When God chose Mary for his instrument, when God
himself in the manger at Bethlehem decided to come into
this world, that was no romantic family portrait, but the
beginning of a total turning point, a new ordering of all
things on this earth. If we want to participate in this
Advent and Christmas happening, we cannot simply be
like spectators at a theater performance, enjoying all the
familiar scenes, but we must ourselves become part of
this activity, which is taking place in this "changing of
all things." We must have our part in this drama. The
spectator becomes an actor in the play. We cannot with-
draw ourselves from it.

What part then do we play? Pious shepherds who bow the knee? Kings, who bring their gifts? What play then is being performed when Mary becomes the mother of God? When God comes in the lowly state of a child in the manger? It is the judgment of the world and the salvation of the world that is being acted out here. And it is the Christ child in the manger, who judges and saves the world. He turns back the great and the powerful. He has brought down the thrones of the rulers. He has humbled the proud. He has used his power against the high and mighty, and has raised up the lowly and made them great and glorious in his compassion. And therefore we cannot approach this manger as we approach the cradle of any other child. But who would go to this manger goes where something will happen. When he leaves the manger, he leaves either condemned or delivered. Here, he will be broken in pieces or know the compassion of God coming to him.

What does that mean? Isn't it all rhetoric, pastoral exaggeration, a beautiful, pious legend? What does it mean that such things are spoken of the Christ child? If you take this as mere rhetoric, then you will celebrate Advent and Christmas in the pagan way that you always have. But to us, this is no mere rhetoric. For what is true is that God himself, the Lord and Creator of all things, here becomes little and helpless, here in a corner, in seclusion, unnoticed, he enters the world. Helpless and powerless as a baby, he meets us and wants to be with us. This is not trifling or playing games, but real! The Christ child indicates to us where he is and who he is and from this place judges all human pretensions to greatness, dethroning the rulers and devaluing the proud.

The throne of God in the world is not as human thrones, but is in the depths of the human soul, in the manger. Around his throne, there are not flattering courtiers, but obscure, unknown, unrecognizable forms, who cannot see enough of this wonder and gladly live from God's mercy alone.

There are only two places where the powerful and great in this world lose their courage, tremble in the depth of their souls, and become truly afraid. These are the manger and the cross of Jesus Christ. No man of violence dares to approach the manger, even King Herod did not risk that. For it is here that thrones tumble, the mighty fall, and the high and mighty ones are put down, because God is with the lowly. Here the rich are nobodies, because God is with the poor and the hungry. "He fills the hungry with good things but has sent the rich away empty." Before the Virgin Mary, before the manger of Christ, before God in his lowly state, the rich have no rights and no hope. They are convicted. The proud man may think that nothing will happen to him today, yet tomorrow or the day after, it will happen. God brings down tyrants from their thrones. God lifts up the humble. For this purpose, Jesus Christ as the child in the manger, as the son of Mary, has come into the world.

In eight days, we shall celebrate Christmas and now for once let us make it really a festival of Christ in our world. Then we must prepare ourselves by getting rid of something which plays a great role in our lives. We must be clear about how, in the face of the manger, we shall think about what is high and what is low in human life in the future. Of course, we are not all powerful, even if we wish we were and we reluctantly admit it. Only a few are really powerful. But there are many more with little power, who when they can, exert what power they have, and live with one thought: that they might have greater power! God's thoughts are the opposite. He desires to be even lower, in humble state, unnoticed, in self-forgetfulness, in insignificance, in worthlessness, not wishing to be high. And it is on this road that we meet with God himself. Everyone of us lives side by side with some whom we call great, and some whom we call low. Every one of us has someone who is below us. Is it possible that this Christmas we could rethink this radical point, learning and knowing that our way, insofar as it is the way to God, leads us not to the high and mighty, but really into the depths, to the humble and poor? And that every way of life, which is only a way up higher must end in disaster?

God is not mocked. It is not a light thing to God that every year we celebrate Christmas and do not take it seriously. His word holds and is certain. When he comes in his glory and power into the world in the manger, he will put down the mighty from their seats, unless ultimately, ultimately they repent.

It is a very important matter for a congregation that they understand this point and that they see the consequences for their life together.

There is much to think about here about the direction this congregation is taking.

Who of us would want to celebrate Christmas correctly? Who will finally lay at the manger all power, all honor, all reputation, all vanity, all pride, and all selfishness? Who is content to be lowly and to let God alone be high? Who sees the glory of God in the humble state of the child in the manger? Who says with Mary: "The Lord has been mindful of my humble state. My soul praises the Lord and my spirit rejoices in God my Savior?" Amen.[4]

Finkenwalde:
The Preacher's
Seminary

1935 - 1937

WHILE IN LONDON, BONHOEFFER WAS INVOLVED in the church struggle in Germany, the ecumenical movement, his pastorate, and plans which he had long nurtured to go to India and learn from Mahatma Gandhi. The Bishop of Chichester had written to Gandhi about Bonhoeffer's desire to join him for a period. But since his university days, he had gradually come to the conclusion that his greatest pleasure and his real vocation was teaching and writing theology. The universities in Germany were dominated by the German Christians—so far as theology was concerned. The Confessing Church, however, was making plans for theological seminaries under their own control. One such seminary was the Berlin-Brandenburg of the Confessing Church of the Old Prussian Union and Niemöller proposed Bonhoeffer to be its director.

Plans for India were abandoned, but Bonhoeffer asked for time to visit communities in England before leaving. He was deeply impressed by the community of Anglicans at Mirfield and there he learned to pray Psalm 119, which he continued to do. He also visited Kelham and the Oxford Fathers, as well as seminaries of other denominations. He was deeply impressed by the Methodist Theological College at Richmond.

Eberhard Bethge comments: "The closer this new task approached, the more it became a focal point for everything which had preoccupied Bonhoeffer in recent years: a theology of the Sermon on the Mount, a community of service and spiritual exercise, a witness to passive resistance, and ecumenical openness."[1]

Bonhoeffer accepted the invitation and left his London pastorates. In April he was ready, but there was difficulty in finding a building for the new "preaching seminary." At last, they were offered the use of the Rhineland Bible School on the Baltic Sea until the beginning of the summer season. On April 26, 1935, the candidates and their director, who was of much the same age as they were, "made their way to the cabins among the dunes on the Baltic coast." There were twenty-three candidates, but it took some days before they all arrived and moved into their cabins. In the summer, the seminary was moved to a more suitable building in Finkenwalde, not far from Stettin. It was an empty house, yet to find furniture when Bonhoeffer gave his first lecture there on June 26. On the Sunday before Advent (Totensonntag), Bonhoeffer preached on Revelation 14:6–13, which I have included as an Advent sermon in 1935. There are no Advent sermons during this period; at least none have survived. There are, however, three funeral sermons, which gave Bonhoeffer the opportunity to preach about death, one of the central themes of Advent. The first of these is included in this section.

November 24, 1935
Remembrance Sunday

Who and What is Babylon?

Then I saw another angel flying in midair, and he had the eternal gospel to proclaim to those who live on the earth—to every nation, tribe, language and people. He said in a loud voice, "Fear God and give him glory, because the hour of his judgment has come. Worship him who made the heavens, the earth, the sea and the springs of water."

A second angel followed and said, "Fallen! Fallen is Babylon the Great, which made all the nations drink the maddening wine of her adulteries." A third angel followed them and said in a loud voice: "If anyone worships the beast and his image and receives his mark on the forehead or on the hand, he, too, will drink of the wine of God's fury, which has been poured full strength into the cup of his wrath. He will be tormented with burning sulfur in the presence of the holy angels and of the Lamb. And the smoke of their torment rises for ever and ever. There is no rest day or night for those who worship the beast and his image, or for anyone who receives the mark of his name." This calls for patient endurance on the part of the saints who obey God's commandments and remain faithful to Jesus.

Then I heard a voice from heaven say, "Write: Blessed are the dead who die in the Lord from now on."

"Yes," says the Spirit, "they will rest from their labor, for their deeds will follow them."

Revelation 14:6–13

"And I saw." The curtain is rent asunder and John is able to see what is hidden from our eyes, the world after death. So much is quite clear: This world is everything but dead. It is to the highest degree, living, full of activity, full of faces, full of words, full of agony and of blessing. The world after death is alive to the fullest extent. It is not a nothing, not a fading away which awaits us when at last we close our eyes, but an undreamed of happening that we encounter. No one is comforted with false hopes: Death is soon all over. Or rather, let us say: Soon all begins, we become more serious, more critical of ourselves. Our text will help us to become ready for that other world. How can we Christians, Christ's people, learn to face death? That is the question and our text gives the answer. It is a threefold message of joy, which is proclaimed today from that world, as comfort this Remembrance Sunday, as a help to face death.

"Then I saw another angel flying in mid-air, and he had the eternal gospel to proclaim." Where today shall we find the visionaries who can see the angel of God?

They are no longer with us. If they were, they would see the heavens open to reveal a new world. Through the heavens, the angel flies with the eternal gospel. That belongs in the midst of heaven, as it also belongs on the earth, the eternal gospel. This is a great comfort for all who believe: The gospel remains. It is an eternal gospel, our gospel, which we hear, read and preach, Sunday by Sunday, the gospel that once changed our lives, when we understood it for the first time. By many mocked and derided, and thrown into the dust. Yet, hidden and dearly loved, confessed by martyrs through the ages, by confessors and unnumbered souls. The gospel remains through all eternity. We need not fear or trouble ourselves with the thought that it might, as it seems today, be abandoned. What are ten years or even more of our experience and observations? The gospel is eternal and remains despite everything. It remains the one and only true proclamation of God and his lordship over the world.

And though there be thousands of religions and views and opinions and philosophies in the world, and though they construct the most attractive of ideologies, and though the hearts of the people are moved and won over by them, they are all shattered by death. They must all be broken because they are not true. Only the gospel remains. And before the end comes, it will be preached to every nation, tribe, language, and people, throughout the whole world. Although it may appear that there are many ways, there is really only one true way for all people on the earth: the gospel.

And the speech of the angel is so simple that anyone could understand it: "Fear God and give him glory, because the hour of his judgment is come. Worship him who made the heavens, the earth, the sea, and the springs of water." That is the first command of the gospel. "Fear God" and you will have nothing else to fear. Don't fear what the next day may bring. Don't fear other people. Don't fear violence and power, even when it comes to you personally and can rob you of your life. Don't fear the high and mighty in the world. Don't fear yourself. Don't fear your sins. All these fears will die. From all these fears you will be set free. For you they are no longer there. But fear God and him alone. For he has the power over all the powers of this world. The whole world is in fear of God. He has power to give us life or to destroy us. All other powers are a mere game. God alone is real, seriously real. Fear God seriously and "give him the glory." He would be acknowledged as the creator, as our creator; he would be acknowledged as the reconciler, who has made peace between God and man; he would be acknowledged as redeemer, who at the end sets us free from all our sins and all our burdens. Honor him and his holy gospel, "because the hour of his judgment is come." And this judgment is the gospel itself. The eternal gospel is the judge of all peoples.

On that day of judgment, when we appear before him, what will he ask of us? God the judge will ask us only one question: Have you believed and obeyed the gospel? He will not ask whether we were German or Jew, whether we were National Socialists or not, whether we belonged to the Confessing Church or not, whether we were great and influential and successful or not, whether we have a life's work to show, whether we were honored among the people or lowly, unimportant, failures and unrecognized. In that day, God will ask everyone whether they put their trust in the gospel for their survival. The gospel alone will be our judge. By the gospel, souls will be divided in eternity. If we know that and see how the gospel is misused among us, in the world, and also in the church, we have good reason to be afraid. Then we need to see the first vision that John saw and take note. An eternal gospel, which is eternally proclaimed to all peoples, the eternal judge over all peoples. An eternal gospel, that is the one and only remaining comfort for the community of believers. That is the message of joy for all who yet must die.

"A second angel followed and said, 'Fallen! Fallen is Babylon the Great, which made all the nations drink the maddening wine of her adulteries.'" John saw that. And he also saw the other side, that Babylon was still great, mighty, and powerful; that Babylon stands there, still invincible and all the peoples tremble before her and bow down. Babylon, the enemy of God, the city which does not cease to build her towers up into the heavens.

Babylon, the Anti-Christ, who defies the crucified Lord by its own power, who destroys the people with blasphemous and seductive words, as the harlot who makes her victim drunk with strong wine, so as to bemuse and confuse and seduce him with all kinds of devilries and godless splendors. Babylon, whom the people idolize, love, all unaware that they are walking unconsciously into the net. Babylon, who longs for nothing but subservience, sex, and drunkenness, which take away their senses and lead men to wild passions. Who would venture to say of this Babylon, that it will not last, but will fall! With what nervousness must the Christian community, who will not be citizens of this state, who must live and suffer outside of it, look upon that city from the outside! With what prayers must they earnestly pray for it, pray for its downfall! Who is Babylon? Was it Rome? Who is it today? We are not prepared to risk an answer to that question yet? Not because we are afraid of men! But the church does not yet know. And yet it sees frightful things beginning to unfold. And now, the voice from heaven, the message of joy, for the community of believers, is heard: "Fallen! Fallen! Is Babylon the Great."

It is already accomplished. The judgment has already gone forth from God. Babylon is already condemned.

Babylon cannot stand, because it can no longer stand before God. Therefore, fear not Babylon, for it can no longer harm you. It is already condemned. It is already as though it were gone up in smoke, now dust and ashes, a ruined city. So, no longer think of it as a serious threat. Therefore do not be consumed with hate or envy for her. It is all so transient, so transient. It no longer has any significance at all. But quite other things are significant. Hold fast to your faith. Hold fast to Christ. Don't let yourself be troubled by Babylon, be sober, and don't let fear overcome you. Attend to the voice of God, which says, "Fallen! Fallen is Babylon the Great." The voice of God, the Almighty alone is important and true. It is that which leads you to life. When Babylon is destroyed, death and judgment are also destroyed. Babylon is fallen, rejoice community of believers! That is the second message of joy for the community which must face death.

"A third angel followed them and said in a loud voice: 'If anyone worships the beast and his image and receives his mark on the forehead or on his hand, he too will drink of the wine of God's fury.'" The beast is the lord of Babylon, the man of blasphemy, of pride, and of violence. And that is the worst. The beast is never satisfied until all people submit to him and even then he requires that they are branded with his name on forehead and hand, that he may be sure that they belong to him in thought and deed.

The beast must be worshiped. As Christians sign themselves with the sign of the cross, so the beast desires that all who belong to him should sign themselves with the evil sign of blasphemy. And they pray to the beast and say: Who is greater and mightier than thee, O beast? Who will stand against you? Who is more powerful and godlike? The names of those who pray to the beast are not written in the book of life. Before God and Christ they are neither pleasing, nor chosen, but are a blasphemy to God.

"He . . . will drink of the wine of God's fury, which has been poured full strength into the cup of his wrath. He will be tormented with burning sulphur in the presence of the holy angels and of the Lamb. And the smoke of their torment rises forever and ever. There is no rest day or night for those who worship the beast and his image, or for anyone who receives the mark of his name." A burning, unmixed wine is the fury of God which a blasphemer feels within the very marrow of his bones.

Inexpressibly terrible are the things named here. Nothing worse could be added. How can such a message be a source of joy for us? ". . . tormented with burning sulphur in the presence of the holy angels and of the Lamb."

They must see the Christ whom they have denied in their torment. "And the smoke of their torment rises forever and ever. There is no rest day or night." Let us not rejoice in the face of such words, but be still. And within ourselves consider and say: "God be merciful to me a sinner and grant us all thy salvation, thou who alone deserves honor. Thou alone art just. Thou hast given us peace in the presence of our enemies. Thou alone art our comfort and our joy!"

No, in the face of God's terrible judgment upon the world, we shall not break out in cries of triumph, but plead: God give patience to thy saints in all our impatience. Give obedience to thy church in thy command to love in all our disobedience. Give us faith in Jesus in all our faithlessness so that when you come and enter into us and support us, then you may also say to us: "Here is patient endurance on the part of the saints who obey God's commandments and remain faithful to Jesus." God, this is all thy grace.

We can now begin to grasp the fact that, in the face of this temptation to impatience and faithlessness, even hate, that it is a mercy to die, to be taken away from it all. Who among us knows that he will hold fast? Who among us knows that he will withstand the last temptation? Therefore, "Blessed are the dead who die in the Lord from now on." "Blessed are the dead." We need to understand that, not from weariness, nor because they are tired of life, but the fear of not holding fast the faith until the end and the joy of knowing that we die in grace. "Blessed are the dead . . . from now on." From such time on, when the power of Babylon and the beast over-reaches itself. But not all the dead are blessed, only those who "die in the Lord," who have learned to die ready for the Lord, who held fast to their faith in Jesus unto the last hour, whether under the suffering of open martyrdom, or in the martyrdom of loneliness, hidden from the public eye. The promise, the blessing for the dead, the resurrection is only for the church of Jesus Christ. Those who belong to her; and those who apart from the church have claim to the promise, fall into the arms of God. "Blessed are the dead who die in the Lord." To die in Christ. Our prayer this day must be that grace be given us that our last hour be not a weakening, that we die as believing Christians, whether old or young, whether quickly or after long years of suffering, whether calm or torn from the lordship of Babylon, or quiet and softly, that our last word be "Christ."

"Yes," says the Spirit, "they will rest from their labor, for their deeds will follow them." And then comes rest from our labor, that means from tribulations, sins, and temptations, which today we experience. No fear anymore of weakening, no fear of sin or the power of Babylon. Then comes rest, because we shall recognize Christ as our Lord and see him. "Their deeds will follow them."

They do not lead us to Jesus—that is by faith alone—
but the deeds follow, which have been done, in God in
Christ for which he has prepared us from the beginning
of the world. Here, we do not know that. Here they are
hidden. They are the works, of which the left hand
knows nothing, while the right hand does them. But they
remain with us, because they belong to us as the everlasting gifts of God.

Lord, teach thy church to die, through thy gospel.
Give us strength to hold fast until you call. We would
gladly behold thine eternal gospel. Amen.[2]

A Funeral Oration

On January 15, 1936, Bonhoeffer preached at the funeral
of his grandmother, Julie Bonhoeffer (née Tafel), who was
ninety-three years old. She came from a revolutionary
family. The Tafels had a wild reputation and it was not
lost on Julie. Dietrich had a special relationship with her
as early as his time as a young student in Tübingen, where
she lived. On April 1, 1933, she marched through a cor-
don of Nazi Stormtroops (S.A.) to shop at a Jewish store,
in defiance of the Nazi boycott of all Jewish establish-
ments that day. She was already ninety. Throughout her
life she closely followed the political world and supported
Dietrich, who was often in correspondence with her.

At her funeral, he preached on Psalm 90.

Lord, you have been our dwelling place
throughout all generations.
Before the mountains were born
or you brought forth the earth and the world,
from everlasting to everlasting you are God.
You turn men back to dust,
saying, "Return to dust, O sons of men."
For a thousand years in your sight
are like a day that has just gone by,
or like a watch in the night.
You sweep men away in the sleep of death;
they are like the new grass of the morning—
though in the morning it springs up new,
by evening it is dry and withered.
We are consumed by your anger
and terrified by your indignation.
You have set our iniquities before you,
our secret sins in the light of your presence.
All our days pass away under your wrath;
we finish our years with a moan.
The length of our days is seventy years—
or eighty if we have the strength;
yet, their span is but trouble and sorrow,
for they quickly pass, and we fly away.
Who knows the power of your anger?
For your wrath is as great as the fear that is due you.

Teach us to number our days aright,
     that we may gain a heart of wisdom.

Psalm 90:1–12

Today, we stand at the grave of our beloved grandmother with deep thankfulness. God's hand has been kindly to us, that he has allowed us to be with her so long. It is difficult to think of our own life without her. She belonged so completely to us, that she will continue to belong. And God's hand was kindly to her right up to the end. He did not leave her to be alone at the very end. He allowed her to see children, grandchildren, and great grandchildren. In her illness, which was severe, he gave her a few days in which she seemed happy and well. She celebrated Christmas only a few weeks ago with the whole household, as she had done so many times before. With great clarity and love, she was able to take part in everything to the very last, a liveliness which moved us all. She spoke with all those around her and had questions for each, giving good wishes and loving greetings to all. God also gave her the clarity to see those around her and the strength to communicate with them. And if today we are sad that she is no longer with us, we should not forget these mercies and be thankful.

"Lord, you have been our dwelling-place through all generations," (the German has Zuflucht, which means "Refuge"). In so long a life, there are times when one must learn the need for a "refuge." And she knew this on several occasions. Quite young, she lost her father. As a mother she knew the sorrow of losing two of her children. Three of her grandchildren fell in the war. As she grew older, her family of the same generation died. Then, shortly before her death, her eldest son, Otto, was taken. God has often visibly intervened in her life and she had to learn again what she had known from childhood: "Lord, you have been our refuge through all generations." And further, "Before the mountains were born or you brought forth the earth and the world, from everlasting to everlasting you are God."

Even in her last illness she held fast to that truth. Accepting what the will of God sends; bearing what is imposed upon her; looking reality in the face, confident and clear; doing what was necessary and commanded; silent and without complaint when much was taken from her, wherein no other person could help, and in all things, bearing herself with great inner happiness and a powerful "Yes" to life—in this manner she understood and conducted her life, in this way she died, and in this way we loved her.

"You turn men back to dust, saying, 'Return to dust, O sons of men.'" (The German has, "You let men die and say, Return, children of men!")

She has seen this return in three generations, and that was her great joy in life. For her children, grandchildren, and great grandchildren she was always there; she always had time for all of them, peace and quiet and good counsel. And although she lived as any other person, her judgments and her counsel always came from a wide experience, from incomparable understanding of human affairs and from a great love. And while she saw the generations come and grow, she was herself quite ready to go. In all her experience and wisdom, one could trace that it was borne with a humble recognition of the limitations of human knowledge, judgment, and life.

"For a thousand years in your sight are like a day that has just gone by . . . The length of our days is seventy years—or eighty if we have the strength; yet their span is but trouble and sorrow."

She was ninety-three years old and she has bequeathed to us the inheritance of another age. With her passes a world which we all carry within us and which we want to carry. The inflexibility of law, the free word of free men, the binding quality of the given word, plain and sober speech, honesty and simplicity in personal and public life—this she believed in with all her heart. She experienced in her own life that it was only with trouble and care that she could make these ideals come true. She did not shy away from this trouble and care. She could not keep silent when she saw these principles betrayed, where she saw human rights violated. Therefore her last years were deeply troubled by the great sorrow she bore for the suffering and fate of the Jews among our people. She sought to help and suffered with them. She stemmed from a different age, out of a different spiritual world. This world does not sink with her into the grave. This inheritance is our obligation and for this we thank her.

But it is not only from her life that we can learn, but in fact also from her death.

"Teach us to number our days aright that we may gain a heart of wisdom." (The German has, "Teach us to consider our days, that we must die that we may be wise"). Such a meaningful, wise life stands also under the limitations of death, which all humankind must bear. We too must eventually go, with all our ideals, our principles, and our work. It will be wise, therefore, to view our life from its limits, from its end; but much more to know of what lies beyond that limit, of the God who is from everlasting to everlasting, into whose hands we fall, whether we wish it or not, into whose hands she is now fallen. What else shall we say of this fulfilled and rich life? We call upon God, our refuge, to whom we can flee in all times of sorrow and trouble: Jesus Christ, in whom there is all truth, righteousness, all freedom, and love. We call upon God who has overcome all hate, all lack of love, and all that disturbs our peace to accept us by his overwhelming love on the cross of Jesus Christ. We pray that what is here veiled and hidden under sin and death may be revealed in eternity, that in peace and clarity we may behold the eternal face of God in Jesus Christ.

And now we do not wish to be sorrowful anymore. That was not her way. She never wanted to make a person sorrowful. We must go back to our work and our daily activity. That is what she knew and expected. She was devoted to her activities and her daily tasks. Therefore we go from her grave strengthened. Strengthened by her example, her life, and her death. Strengthened much more by her faith in God who is her and our refuge from everlasting to everlasting, strengthened by Jesus Christ.

"And the Lord, our God, be gracious unto us and establish the work of our hands; yes, the work of our hands he will establish." Amen.[3]

The Collective
Pastorates

1938-1940

THE YEAR 1937 WAS DISASTROUS for the Confessing Church. The net tightened around them as one after the other of the leaders was arrested. Martin Niemöller was imprisoned for the next eight years. The activities of those who would not conform to the official National Church were severely curtailed. Consequently, at the end of September 1937, the Gestapo closed Finkenwalde.

The Council of Brethren (the organizing body of the Confessing Church) protested their right to train their own ordinands, but in vain. After some discussion, it was decided to form "Collective Pastorates." This placed ordinands in the charge of a friendly pastor, as student pastors, in training with the incumbent. Necessity required remote pastorates in Pomerania—first, Köslin and Schlawe, moving later into remoter parts, ending with Sigurdshof.

Courses of study were continued with Bonhoeffer and Bethge moving around. This situation continued from 1938—1940, when Sigurdshof was finally closed. The students were called up for military service.

Bonhoeffer's Preaching and Commentary

During these two years, Bonhoeffer had no fixed abode and no desk at which to continue his work. He moved between Köslin and Schlawe at first until these places were closed to him and his students. From pillar to post they ended in Sigurdshof, which was closed on March 17, 1940. This gave him no further opportunity for public preaching, with the one exception of August 3, 1941, at a funeral service. Otherwise his preaching and commentaries, his teaching, and his devotional guidance had to be in written form, which he distributed despite the ban imposed upon circulars. Some of his writing was for the daily readings provided by the Moravians in their devotional diaries called "Losungen" (i.e., lozenges to be taken day by day). Others were sermon outlines for students, short commentaries, and lecture notes. One complete text of a sermon has survived which he circulated to his ordinands for their use.

Background Events

During this period a drama was being played out on the world stage. The opponents of the Nazi philosophy watched with horror as Hitler succeeded in deceiving Chamberlain and Daladier at Münich. They had expected that a coup would have overthrown the regime in Germany if Hitler had failed at Münich. Then Czechoslovakia, Poland, and war!

With such a drama, the Advent theme was never far from his message.

The Selection of Materials

There are two undated commentaries, clearly intended for preaching at Advent. There is also a sermon, written for the Sunday after New Year's 1940, which develops the Christmas theme, entitled "The Cross over the Manger."

Advent

The Beautiful Radiance of God

The Mighty One, God, the LORD,
   speaks and summons the earth
   from the rising of the sun to the place where it sets.
From Zion, perfect in beauty,
   God shines forth.
Our God comes and will not be silent;
   a fire devours before him,
   and around him a tempest rages.
He summons the heavens above,
   and the earth, that he may judge his people:
"Gather to me my consecrated ones,
   who made a covenant with me by sacrifice."

Psalm 50:1 – 5

1. "The mighty one, God, the Lord, speaks and summons the earth"—as on the first day of creation he called

it into being. Incessantly, he commands his creation. Thus, he loves his work by his word and his command.

2. But who can recognize him amidst the awesome splendor of nature? Where will you read his name? You must simply confess your faith: the creation remains dumb. God certainly speaks to the world, but not to you. He comes to you from a different direction: from Zion! It is here only that he allows you to see his friendliness and his glory. Here he shines upon you like the morning light after the darkness of the night. In Zion, the chosen place of his dwelling, the place of his promise and his faithfulness. It is here that the Creator manifests himself. Grace and compassion are his glory, friendliness his beautiful radiance.

3. In his radiance, the creator God is our God. He who summons the world, comes out of Zion as our God. He is our God in that he does not keep silent, but speaks to us. He does not speak to us in the same way as he speaks to nature. The radiance that shines forth at Bethlehem is the way God speaks to us.

4. As he places a flaming sword in front of paradise (Gen 3:24), as Jacob must wrestle with the angry God at Jabbok (Gen 32:25–27), so the devouring fire goes before him. In the same way the Baptist goes before Christ. Thus he comes to his saints and summons them to judgment. The message of Advent and of Christmas also is a terrible message: "May Jesus Christ be praised . . . Kyrie eleison!"

5. Does he come to his saints, then, in judgment? Yes! You alone have I known! "It is time for judgment to begin with the family of God" (1 Peter 4:17). Lightening strikes the highest trees first. For God's saints become holy by judgment and the kindness of the Lord. It is only by way of the flaming sword of the angel that one comes into the Promised Land. It is only through judgment that the grace, the radiance of forgiveness, and the kindness of God shines.

6. "Gather to me my consecrated ones, who made a covenant with me through sacrifice." The saints are consecrated by the sacrifice of the cross. In the background of Advent stands the cross of judgment. Here in this sacrifice judgment and kindness are made one.

7. As at Christmas the heavens opened and on Good Friday those same heavens darkened, so also in this Psalm, all creation must serve "his people." That is the purpose. All other words of creation must serve the Word from Zion. Once God has come into the midst of his people, then the judgment of God over all creation will be openly declared. Then it will be clear that this judgment, which began in Bethlehem, was fulfilled in Golgotha. Heaven and earth bows down before him. Christ is then the judge of all the earth.[1]

Advent
Lift Up Your Heads

"There will be signs in the sun, moon and stars. On the earth, nations will be in anguish and perplexity at the roaring and tossing of the sea. Men will faint from terror, apprehensive of what is coming on the world, for the heavenly bodies will be shaken. At that time they will see the Son of Man coming in a cloud with power and great glory. When these things begin to take place, stand up and lift up your heads, because your redemption is drawing near."

He told them this parable: "Look at the fig tree and all the trees. When they sprout leaves, you can see for yourselves and know that summer is near. Even so, when you see these things happening, you know that the kingdom of God is near.

"I tell you the truth, this generation will certainly not pass away until all these things have happened. Heaven and earth will pass away, but my words will never pass away.

"Be careful, or your hearts will be weighed down with dissipation, drunkenness and the anxieties of life, and that day will close on you unexpectedly like a trap . . . Be always on the watch, and pray that you may be able to escape all that is about to happen, and that you may be able to stand before the Son of Man."

Luke 21:25–36

1. Johann Christoph Blumhardt (nineteenth-century Pietist in Wurttemberg) relates how he kept a new carriage in his parish grounds, which would be used for the first time by the Lord Christ when he comes, "then, I will drive him in it." How certain the waiting Blumhardt was about the coming of Christ! How he planned his daily life so that he would be ready for that moment! His mind was fixed upon how he would fare at that moment when he stood before the Lord Jesus. Such certainty is something unknown to us. There is nothing certain, not even our death is certain. Only the second coming of Christ is certain. This faith of Blumhardt is great, but it is too small for the second coming of Christ. For when it happens, the world will not appear as it now appears. The whole creation will be shaken and changed. Sun, moon, and stars will be displaced from their orbits. When God comes to earth, the stars must lose their light before him. The earth itself will be shattered. Creation reaches out towards him. It feels itself dissolving before him. The sea roars and tosses in anguish and joy. And if the universe knows him, how much more will human beings whose Savior and Judge he is. They will in the same manner be aroused when he comes, fearful of the things that are about to happen. Judgment will be over the whole of humankind when he comes to bring the old world to an end.

2. Only on one place in the earth will it be quite different. There will not be anguish at that place, but joy,

not fear, but heads will be held high: that place is the congregation of Christ's people. They know he comes to redeem them. They are like miners who have been trapped in the depths of the mine, who have suffered long, shut up in the dark, who hear the knocking and the breaking down of walls coming closer. Is it the final caving-in of the mine or is the rescuer coming? "Lift up your heads because your redemption is drawing near." For Christians this world is like a fetter, it is too narrow for them. "Dearest Lord Jesus, why do you wait so long? Come, Lord! Here on earth, I am so frightened." The earth, its suffering and temptation makes us anxious, but Christ makes us glad, he brings redemption.

3. When will it happen? If we knew that it would be tomorrow—how would we prepare ourselves? Jesus said that the signs are there that should happen in your lifetime; therefore prepare yourselves and be ready! Was Jesus mistaken? If we take verse 32 literally, then he was. But should we not be thankful that he said it could come as soon as tomorrow? Because he thus calls us to repentance and gives us more time to change our ways? That is the meaning of the verse: be ready! Even today! If he had left us time, we would remain unchanged. It all happens quickly. But the word of Jesus remains forever. Therefore be converted! The time of redemption is near!

4. What should we do if it were to happen tomorrow? We would prepare ourselves with prayer and watchful

awareness. We would be sober and avoid excess. What would food and drink, pleasure and desire mean then? In a moment they are gone and cannot reach into eternity. Perhaps for a short time we would hold to a discipline of life. Would you not want to lose the world with its sorrows and anxieties in order to be worthy to stand before the Son of Man? For one who has waited for him, nothing else is longed for. The one who has waited like Blumhardt. Like every true Christian community has waited for him and rejoiced at his coming. Like the bride rejoicing at the coming of her bridegroom. For the waiting church the day of Jesus' coming is a great day of rejoicing.[2]

The Cross Over the Manger

[Text of a sermon written for the
first Sunday after New Year 1940]

When they had gone, an angel of the Lord appeared to Joseph in a dream. "Get up," he said, "take the child and his mother and escape to Egypt. Stay there until I tell you, for Herod is going to search for the child to kill him."

So he got up, took the child and his mother during the night and left for Egypt, where he stayed until the death of Herod.

And so was fulfilled what the Lord had said through the prophet: "Out of Egypt I called my son."

When Herod realized that he had been outwitted by the Magi, he was furious, and he gave orders to kill all the boys in Bethlehem and its vicinity who were two years old and under, in accordance with the time he had learned from the Magi. Then what was said through the prophet Jeremiah was fulfilled:

> *A voice is heard in Ramah,*
> *weeping and great mourning,*
> *Rachel weeping for her children*
> *and refusing to be comforted,*
> *because they are no more."*

After Herod died, an angel of the Lord appeared in a dream to Joseph in Egypt and said, "Get up, take the child and his mother and go to the land of Israel, for those who were trying to take the child's life are dead." So he got up, took the child and his mother and went to the land of Israel. But when he heard that Archelaus was reigning in Judea in place of his father Herod, he was afraid to go there. Having been warned in a dream, he withdrew to the district of Galilee, and he went and lived in a town called Nazareth. So was fulfilled what was said through the prophets: "He will be called a Nazarene."

Matthew 2:13–23

My dear congregation! I am sure that you have noticed at the end of these familiar stories—the flight to Egypt, the massacre of the innocents in Bethlehem, and the return of the Holy Family to Nazareth—each time there is a phrase from the Old Testament, and these words are introduced by, "So was fulfilled what was said." We have often passed over these words and thought of them simply as a repeated formula. In this way we have overlooked something important and beautiful in our text.

"So was fulfilled." That means that nothing could happen to Jesus which God had not already determined beforehand. That also means that if we are with Jesus, nothing can happen to us which God has not already decided and promised beforehand. Despite all the thinking, planning, and mistakes that we humans make, even the gruesome hands of the murderous Herod play their part. Finally everything goes the way that God had foreseen, had wanted, and had spoken. God never lets the control go out of his hands. That is a great consolation: God only fulfills what God himself has promised. Anyone who has the Holy Scriptures in his hand and in his heart will again and again have evidence for this great consolation.

The wise men from the East worshiped Jesus and brought him costly gifts. Is it not a shocking contrast that the King of Judah, Herod, should seek the child to kill him. Herod who sits on the throne of David, king and at the same time tyrant over God's people; Herod, who knows the history, the promise, and the hope of this people, plots murder when he hears that God has fulfilled his promises and sends his king of righteousness and truth and peace to his people. The mighty, brutal lords often stained with blood, seek to kill the vulnerable, innocent child because they fear him. All earthly power is on the side of Herod, but God is on the side of the child.

And God has other means than Herod. In a dream he sends his angel to Joseph and tells him to flee to Egypt, beyond the limit of Herod's power. Mysterious as God himself are his means. There never fail powers and servants to make known his ways. Surely, he has given us his Word and there made clear his will. But in special times he has used special means to ensure that we do not lose the right path. Who has not experienced this special help and guidance of God? In the dream of the night, God orders Joseph to fly to Egypt and without a moment's hesitation, Joseph obeys the heavenly instruction and departs with the child and his mother—twice in this brief exchange, the mother and child are named! Should the Word of God be fulfilled and made known to us, we must obey it and if needed we should be prepared to rise in the night to do so. Joseph did just that. The child, Jesus, must fly with his elders. Could God not have protected him from Herod even in Bethlehem? Of course he could, but it is not for us to ask what God can do, but what in fact he wills. God wills that Jesus escapes to Egypt. He indicates also that he can protect Jesus and that nothing will happen to him unless God allows it. Jesus lives now in Egypt, where his people were. In his own body he should live through the sorrows of his people. In Egypt, Israel suffered hardship, in Egypt the hardship of Jesus began. In Egypt, God's people and their king must live in sorrow in a strange land. God led his people out of Egypt into the Promised Land, and from Egypt God called his Son back to Israel. What once the prophet had said about the people of Israel, is now fulfilled in Jesus: "Out of Egypt I called my Son." The flight into Egypt was no blind accident, but divine promise and fulfillment. In Egypt, Jesus would be completely at one with the suffering and joy of his people, God's people, with us. In Egypt, he is with us in a foreign land and with him we also will be brought out from that strange land into the Land of Promise, God's own country. The anger of Herod was great, as the wise men learned and, at the command of God, they did not return to Jerusalem to tell him where Jesus was to be found. With immeasurable agitation and jealousy, Herod now ordered the murder of all the children of Bethlehem under the age of three. He thought that in this way he would be sure to catch the divine child. But clever and gruesome as this massacre was, it failed in its objective. Herod wanted to get rid of the Christ, but Christ lived on and in his place the children were massacred for him. The innocent children of Bethlehem died to protect the life of their Lord and King who was the same age as they were. They were the first martyrs of Christendom, witnesses dying to save the life of Jesus Christ, their Savior. All persecution has as its aim to get rid of Jesus Christ, to kill the Christ child, but it can never harm him. Christ lives, and with him are the martyrs of all time.

When the Lord Jesus Christ is pursued and persecuted, great suffering, crying, groaning, and howling come over the people, as in Bethlehem when the innocent children had to die. Again and again, when the people of God are in trouble and distress, tears flow. So it was in the time of Rachel, the mother of the people of Israel, whose grave lies near to Bethlehem, Rachel weeping for all her children. It was in the last days of Jerusalem before it fell to the Babylonians, when the prophet Jeremiah looked down upon the tragedy and wept. But it was now, when the mothers of Bethlehem wept for their children, for whom Jesus Christ died, that the full meaning of the prophet's words were revealed:

> *A voice is heard in Ramah,*
> *mourning and great weeping,*
> *Rachel weeping for her children*
> *and refusing to be comforted,*
> *because her children are no more.*
> Jeremiah 31:15

The weeping over the witness unto death of Jesus Christ rises and will not be silenced throughout time, until the end. It is the weeping over the world, estranged from God and hostile to Christ, over the blood of the innocent, over the world's own guilt and sin, for whom Jesus Christ himself came to suffer. But in the midst of all this inconsolable weeping, there is a great consolation: Jesus Christ lives and we will live with him, if we suffer with him.

The massacre of the innocents in Bethlehem, for all its godless horror, must ultimately serve God in bringing his promises to fulfillment. Suffering and tears come over God's people. But they are costly to God, because Christ has gathered them to himself of his own will and Christ takes them and carries them into eternity.

Day after day and year after year, Joseph awaited the divine command to return home. Joseph will not take this decision himself. Joseph waits upon God's wisdom. Then God sends the command in the dream of the night, to stand up and go home with the child and his mother, ". . . those who were trying to take his child's life are dead." The mighty Herod is dead without achieving his purpose. But Jesus lives. So has it always been in the history of the Church. First distress, persecution, fear of death for the children of God, for the disciples of Jesus Christ. But then came the time when it is said, " . . . those who were trying to take the child's life are dead." Nero is dead, Diocletian is dead, the enemies of Luther and the Reformation are dead, but Jesus lives, and with him, those who belong to him. The times of persecution come to an end and the truth emerges—Jesus lives!

The child Jesus returns to the land of Israel, at God's call. Jesus comes to claim his kingdom and to mount his throne. Joseph brings Jesus first to Judea, where the King of Israel will wait. But a special divine word delays him and commands him to settle in Nazareth. For the Israelites, Nazareth has a scandalous and unpleasant sound in their ears: "Nazareth! Can anything good come from there?" (John 1:46, Nathanael is speaking). Despite this and perhaps because of it, Jesus grows up there: "So was fulfilled what was said through the prophets, 'He will be called a Nazarene.'" This quotation may prove difficult to understand, because in this form we cannot find it among the prophetic books. We have to learn how to read the biblical text aright. It does not say here that any one particular prophet spoke these words, but that "the prophets" taught. What is meant here, therefore, is that again and again the Old Testament implies that the future King would appear in humility and as one unimpressive. Admittedly, it does not say, "from Nazareth." The evangelist finds this echoed in certain passages of Isaiah, especially Isaiah 11:1, where it reads that, "A shoot will come up from the stump of Jesse; from his roots a branch will bear fruit." A branch, a shoot, an unimpressive twig, and from this weak stump comes the Messiah of Israel, like a twig. The Hebrew word for "twig" is "nezer," the same basic form from which the place name "Nazareth" comes. So deeply hidden, the evangelist finds the promise in the Old Testament that Jesus would be poor, despised, and lowly. It was for Joseph as for all the world incomprehensible that the little regarded Nazareth should be the destination for the Savior of the world. That he should live in poverty, obscurity, and humility was the will of God. With his life of obscurity, despised and rejected, he shares the lot of all the despised of humankind, bearing their sorrows and able to become their Savior. From this story we have learned that God fulfills three great promises in the child Jesus: Jesus experiences the history of God's people in his own body; he brings to those people who belong to him, not only joy, but also suffering and death according to his will; he lives in obscurity and humility in order to be the helper of all people. All this takes place according to the promises of God. It is the fulfillment of the will of God for the salvation of the world.

We are about to enter a new year. Many human plans and failures, much human hostility and distress will certainly accompany our way. But so long as we remain with Jesus and walk with him, we can be certain that nothing can happen to us other than that which God has foreseen, wished, and promised. It is the consolation of a life lived with Jesus that what was said of him will also be true for us: So was fulfilled what the Lord has said. Amen.

Prayer: We praise thee, O Lord, that all things are in thy hand and all is under thy control. Thou leadest those who are thine in Christ safely through all hardship and enmity according to thy will. Into this new year also lead thy church and all its members in the paths of righteousness, according to thy will. Amen.[3]

War—Conspiracy—Prison—Death

1939-1945

As war gathered over Europe like a storm, friends of Dietrich Bonhoeffer feared for his safety and sought to rescue him. They arranged lecture tours in America. Bonhoeffer went, but soon realized he was mistaken. If war came, he reasoned, a Christian in Germany would be faced with a dilemma. If he prayed for the victory of Germany, he was praying for the destruction of civilization. The awful alternative would be to pray for the defeat of his country that civilization might survive. This dilemma, he faced, but he could not do that in the safety of America. He returned to Germany and joined with those who were seeking the overthrow of the Nazi regime. Several professional soldiers had assured him that once the war started, Hitler would easily be defeated because he had no experience of directing a war. Then would be the chance to replace the hated regime with one which their erstwhile enemies would respect and deal with honorably. All this was shattered by the extraordinary success of the German advance in Europe. The turning point came when Paris fell, on June 17, 1940. Bethge reports the way in which Bonhoeffer received the news. They were in Memel together enjoying the sunshine in an open-air café when the loudspeaker announced the fall of Paris and all began to rejoice and raise their arms shouting, "*Deutschland, Deutschland über alles.*" To his surprise, Bethge saw Bonhoeffer raising his arm like the rest, and then saying to Bethge, "Raise your arm! Are you crazy?" and later added, "We shall have to run risks for very different things now, but not for that salute!" Bethge comments, "It was then that Bonhoeffer's double life began: the involvement as a pastor in the political underground movement.'[1]

Such an involvement was foreign to the whole tradition of the Lutheran Church, which recognized the distinction between the authority of the church in things spiritual and that of the state in things political, both, of course, under the authority of God. Later, in 1943, when he wrote from prison, he expressed the view that this involvement "may prevent me from taking up my ministry again later on."[2]

On September 4, 1940, Bonhoeffer was forbidden to speak in public and required to report regularly to the police. He began to concentrate his work on the subject *Ethics*, which occupied him until his death. Life was made a great deal easier when he was appointed to the Abwehr (Military Intelligence), which was not open to the scrutiny of the Gestapo. He was appointed to the Abwehr Office in Münich and resided for some time in the Benedictine Abbey at Ettal in Bavaria. During this time, he had little to do and could devote his energies to studying *Ethics*. By November, he began his overseas visits on behalf of the Abwehr—first to Switzerland and most memorably to Sweden in 1942. The Swiss visit which lasted four weeks brought him again into contact with the World Council of Churches (in process of formation). In Sweden, he met George Bell to discuss a project for the overthrow of the Nazi regime by a group of high-ranking officers and leaders in church and state. It was a request to the British Government to respect any alternative government in Germany that might be formed after the fall of the Nazis. They asked for a sign that there would not be another Versailles, or "unconditional surrender," but a negotiated peace. The request was rejected and the war went on for another three years.

There was great difficulty in getting any precise charge against Bonhoeffer, but he was arrested on April 5, 1943 and remained a prisoner until his death in 1945. He was hanged in Flossenbürg on April 9, 1945.

Before his arrest he wrote and circulated an assessment of the ten years that Hitler had been in power, called, "After Ten Years."[3] Once in prison, he wrote letters—largely to Eberhard Bethge, but also to family and to his fiancée, Maria von Wedemeyer. Our main source of material during this period comes from the unfinished manuscript on *Ethics*, the circular, "After Ten Years," and his *Letters and Papers from Prison*—letters, a sketch for a novel, the beginning of a drama, and ten poems.

In view of the times, the Advent theme is never far away. But this section begins with a sermon, dated Christmas 1940, on the Advent text, Isaiah 9:5–6. As Bonhoeffer had already been forbidden to speak publicly, this was obviously a written sermon, presumably circulated. That Christmas he wrote personally to a hundred colleagues and Finkenwalde students, many of whom were now serving in the army. With his message to them and his greetings, he enclosed a reproduction of Altdorfer's *Holy Family in the Ruined House*.

Christmas 1940

The Government Upon the Shoulders of the Child

For to us a child is born, to us a son is given, and the government will be on his shoulders. And he will be called Wonderful Counselor, Mighty God, Everlasting Father, Prince of Peace. Of the increase of his government and peace there will be no end. He will reign on David's throne and over his kingdom, establishing and upholding it with justice and righteousness from that time on and forever. The zeal of the LORD Almighty will accomplish this.

Isaiah 9:6–7

Amidst disastrous words and signs, which declare the divine anger and terrible punishment for the defeated and near destroyed people; amidst the guilt and distress of the people of God, a voice is heard, gentle and mysterious, but full of blessed confidence, announcing deliverance through the birth of the divine child. It will not be fulfilled for seven hundred years yet. But so deeply is the prophet immersed in the thoughts and decisions of God that he speaks of the future as he sees it already; the child in the manger, Jesus, and he announces the hour of deliverance: "For to us a child is born." What one day will be is already there in the sight of God, sure and certain. It is not only something that one day will happen—deliverance for future generations— but already for the prophet himself and for his generation, yes, for all generations: "For to us a child is born." No human person can speak like that on his own.

We who do not know what will happen next year, how can we comprehend how anyone could see out over hundreds of years? And the times were no less certain then than they are today. Only the Spirit of God, who encompasses the beginning and the end of the world, can in this way reveal the secret of the future to his chosen person. Such prophecy is to strengthen believers and to warn unbelievers. This voice of an individual which rings through the centuries, softly at first, is here and there joined by the voices of other prophets and is heard today in the nightly prayers of the pastor and the joyful celebrations of the believing congregation of Christians: "For to us a child is born, to us a son is given."

This is about the birth of a child, not of the astonishing work of a strong man, not of the bold discovery of a wise man, not of the pious work of a saint. It really is beyond all understanding: the birth of a child shall bring about the great change, shall bring to all mankind salvation and deliverance. What kings and statesmen, philosophers and artists, religious leaders and moral teachers have labored for in vain is now brought about by a newborn child. Here a child, born into the midst of world history, has put to shame the wisdom and efforts of the strong. A child, born of a human mother, a Son given by God. That is the secret of the salvation of the world. All the past and all the future is here encompassed. The unending comfort of the Almighty God comes to us, humbly and in the form of a child, his Son. That this child is born, for us, given for us, that this human child, God's Son, belongs to me, that I know him, have him, love him, that I am his and he is mine, means that now my life depends only on him. A child has our life in his hands.

How shall we deal with such a child? Have our hands, soiled with daily toil, become too hard and too proud to fold in prayer at the sight of this child? Has our head become too full of serious thoughts to be thought through and problems to be solved, that we cannot bow our head in humility before the wonder of this child? Can we not forget all our stress and struggles, our sense of importance, and for once worship the child, as did the shepherds and the wise men from the East, bowing before the divine child in the manger like children? Can we not be like the aged Simeon, who took the child in his arms and saw the fulfillment of all his waiting, and in this moment recognize the fulfillment of our whole life? It is truly a strangely moving sight when a strong, proud man bows the knee before the child, and with childlike heart finds and honors this divine child as his savior. Certainly, it must blow the mind, perhaps give rise to wicked laughter, when there is heard in this old, clever, experienced world of ours, so sure of its knowledge, this proclamation of salvation by Christian believers: "For to us a child is born, to us a son is given, and the government will be on his shoulders." That the government of all the world should lie upon the weak shoulders of this newborn child! This one thing we know: These shoulders will one day bear the weight of the whole world. With the cross, all the sin and the sorrow of this world will be laden upon these shoulders. But his authority will remain, he will not break under the burden, but bring it through triumphantly. The government which lies upon the shoulders of the child in the manger consists of the patient bearing of humanity's burden and its guilt. The bearing of this burden begins in the manger, begins there where the eternal Word of God took to himself human flesh and bore it. Precisely in the lowliness and weakness of the child is the beginning of his taking the government of all the world upon him. The head of the house indicates his government over the house by the key which he hangs over his shoulder. That shows that he has the authority to open or shut the door, to let people in or to show them out, as he will. And that is also the way that the cross over his shoulder shows his authority as governor. He opens to those whose sins he forgives, and he shuts out the proud. That is the nature of this child's government, that he receives the humble, the lowly and sinners, bearing their burden, but he rejects and brings to nothing the proud, the high and mighty, the self-righteous.

Who is this child, of whom the prophets speak and at whose birth heaven and earth rejoice? It is only with stammering tongues that we can speak his name or seek to describe what is embraced by this name. Words limp and stumble when they attempt to say who this child is. Yes, when human lips try to express the name of this child, strange word-pictures emerge, which we do not know: "Wonderful Counselor," "Mighty God," "Everlasting Father," "Prince of Peace." Every title in these words comes from unfathomable depths and taken together they try to encompass one single name: Jesus.

This child is called, "Wonderful Counselor." In him, the wonder of all wonders has taken place. The birth of the Savior-child comes out of the eternal counsel of God. God gave us his Son in the form of a human child. God became man, the Word became flesh. That is the wonder of God's love for us and it is the unfathomable counsel of God which wins and delivers us. And because this child of God is uniquely Wonderful Counselor, he is therefore himself also the source of all wonder and all counsel. Anyone who recognizes Jesus as the Son of God, whose every word and every deed is a wonder, will find in him the profoundest and most helpful counsel in all times of trouble and questioning. Yes, before his lips can speak, he is full of wonder and full of counsel. Go to the child in the manger and you will find in him wonder upon wonder, counsel upon counsel.

This child is called "Mighty God." The child in the manger is none other than God himself. Nothing greater could be said: God becomes a child. In the Jesus-child of Mary dwells Almighty God. Just take that in for a moment! Don't speak, don't think any further! Stand quietly and wait before this statement, that God has become a child! Here, he is poor like us, wretched like us, and helpless like us, a child of flesh and blood like us, our brother. And yet he is God, almighty God. Where is the divinity, where is the power of this child? It is in the divine love by which he becomes like us. His pitiable condition in the manger is his power. In the power of love, he overcomes the chasm between God and man, powerfully overcoming sin and death, he forgives sin and raises from the dead. Kneel low before this pitiable manger, before this child of poor people and speak in faith with stammering tongue, the words of the prophets, "Almighty God," and he will be your God and your power.

"Everlasting Father"—how can this be the name of the child? Only if the everlasting fatherly love of God is revealed in this child and that this child will do nothing other than bring the love of the Father to the earth. In this way, the Father and the Son are one, and he who sees the Son, sees the Father. This child will do nothing of himself, he is not a wonder child in the human sense, but an obedient child of his heavenly Father. At the time of his birth he brought eternity to earth. As Son of God he brings to us all the love of the heavenly Father. Go then to the manger, to seek and find the everlasting Father, who has now become also your loving Father.

"Prince of Peace"—Where God comes to people in love to join with them, peace is established between God and humankind, and also among ourselves, person to person. If you are afraid of the wrath of God, go to the child in the manger and let him give you the peace of God. If you are in strife and hatred with your neighbor, come and see how God, out of his great love, has dealt with your neighbor and will reconcile you both. In the world, power rules. This child is the Prince of Peace. Where he is, peace rules!

"Wonderful Counselor," "Mighty God," "Everlasting Father," "Prince of Peace." This is what we say at the manger in Bethlehem. Our words are confirmed by a glance at the divine child. We try to grasp in phrases what is contained for us in this name: Jesus. Basically, these

words are no more than the unspoken silence of a wor-
shiper in face of the inexpressible reaction to the presence of God in the form of a human child.

We have heard of the birth and the names of the divine
child. Now finally we hear something about his kingdom
(v. 7). The government of this poor child will be great. It
will encompass the whole earth. All generations until the
end of time will serve him whether they know it or not.
His will be a rule over the hearts of all humankind.
Thrones and great kingdoms will be strengthened or broken by this power. The unseen, loving rule of this divine
child over human hearts will be more firmly grounded
than the visible and shining might of earthly lords. And
ultimately all governments on earth must serve the rule
of Jesus Christ over all humankind. Despite all the hostility against it, this government will become greater and
more firmly based. With the birth of Jesus the great kingdom of peace has broken in. Is it not a wonder that when
Jesus has become Lord over all humankind, then peace
rules? Is it not a wonder that the whole earth becoming
Christian means that peace is in the midst of the world?
Only when one does not allow Jesus to rule, then obsti-
nacy, defiance, and hatred express themselves continu-
ously and there can be no peace. Jesus will not establish
his government of peace by force, but only when people
submit to him freely, and allow him to rule over them.
Then he gives to them his wonderful peace. When today,

once again, Christian people are torn apart by war and hate, yes, when even Christian churches cannot come together, that is not the fault of Jesus Christ, but the fault of people who will not allow Jesus to rule over them. This does not mean that the promise is not fulfilled. Peace will have no end when the divine child rules over us.

Jesus Christ "will reign on David's throne and over his kingdom" (v. 7). It is no longer a worldly throne, nor a worldly kingdom, as it once was. But a spiritual throne and a spiritual kingdom. Where is the throne and kingdom of Jesus? It is present there with his Word and sacrament, ruling and governing, in the Church and among his worshipers. In his kingdom, Jesus rules "with justice and righteousness." His justice does not leave unscathed the congregation of believers. No! Precisely on them he executes his strongest judgment and those who are really his people do not seek to avoid it, but bow before it. Jesus can only give a new righteousness once he has judged the sin. His kingdom shall be a kingdom of righteousness, but that cannot be established by us, judging ourselves. It must be divine judgment of our sin. It will be the strength of this kingdom that it rests upon justice and righteousness. This kingdom will continue because justice, the unfulfilled longing of mankind, is made possible with the birth of the divine child. We are called to his kingdom. We can find it if, in the church, among the congregation of believers, we accept the Word and sacrament of the Lord Jesus Christ, if we accept his rule over us, if we recognize the child in the manger as our Savior and Deliverer, allowing him to give us the new life of love. "From that time on" means from the birth of Jesus, "and forever" this kingdom will last. Who can vouch for this, that the storms of world history will not shatter it and bring it to nought, like all other kingdoms? "The zeal of the Lord Almighty will accomplish this." God's zeal for this will guarantee it, that this kingdom shall remain forever. It will in the end bring down all human guilt and all resistance. Whether we are there or not, it will arrive. God himself lays his plans and reaches his objectives, with us or against us. But he wants us to be with him, not by compulsion but willingly. "God with us," "Immanuel," "Jesus"—that is the mystery of this holy night. "For to us a child is born, to us a son is given." I believe that Jesus Christ, truly man, born of a virgin, and also truly God, born of the Father in Heaven, is my Lord.[4]

Ethics—1940
Pomerania and Ettal

As early as 1937, Bonhoeffer was planning a new approach to the problems of Christian ethics. The dimension of evil, which the Nazi regime had uncovered, made traditional ethics inadequate to fight the battles of the day. He thought of this work as the beginning of his life work. In 1939, he had planned to give the Croall lectures in Scotland, at the invitation of John Baillie, but the war intervened. These lectures would have been his magnum opus on "Ethics." In 1940, when he was forbidden to continue with the "Collective Pastorates," he took up work on this plan again. In September and October, this was done in Klein-Krössen but was stopped when he was transferred to Münich. On November 17, 1940, he became a guest at the Benedictine Monastery in Ettal, Bavaria. There he worked at this book. It was never finished, although later in prison he expressed his hope to finish it on release.

In prison on December 15, 1943, he wrote, "Sometimes I think I really have my life more or less behind me now and that all that would remain for me to do would be to finish my *Ethics*." [5]

The book was never finished, but thanks to Eberhard Bethge, who knew Bonhoeffer's thoughts far better than anyone else, we have a version of the book which is as near as possible to what Bonhoeffer intended. [6] I have selected the section on "The Last Things and the Things Before the Last," which appears fundamental to his view of his suggested title: "The Preparing of the Way and the Entering into Possession."

Justification as the Last Word

All Christian living has its origin and existence in one single happening which the Reformation called "justification by grace alone." It is not what the individual is in himself or herself, but what he or she has become by this happening which defines a Christian life. Here we have the length and breadth of human life in a nutshell, gathered together at one point; the whole of life is contained in this event. What happens here? An ultimate act of suffering which cannot be grasped by any human being. The darkness, which from within and without takes human life into the abyss of hopelessness is bound, conquered, and destroyed by the power of the Word of God; in the light of this deliverance, we see God and our neighbor for the first time. The bewildering labyrinth of the life we have lived so far is shattered. We are free for God and our neighbor. We begin to know in our heart that there is a God who loves us, accepts us, and that by our side is a brother or sister, whom God loves as he loves us. Also, we know now that there is a future with the triune God, who is present among his people. Now, the human being has faith, love, and hope. Past and future become as one in the presence of God. The whole of the past is gathered up in the word "forgiveness;" the whole of the future is in the safekeeping of the true God. The sins of the past are sunk into the abyss of the love of God in

Christ Jesus and overcome. The future will be a life with
God, without sin (see 1 John 3:9). Life, then, is revealed
as detached from the temporal and held fast by the eternal, choosing the way of eternal salvation rather than the
ways of the temporal world, as a member of a community and of creation, which sings praises to the triune
God. All this happens with the encounter of Christ with
the human soul. All this is truth and reality in Christ.
Because it is no dream, it is a truly human life, which is
lived in the presence of Christ. From now on, it is no
longer a lost life, but a justified life, justified by grace
alone.

But not only "by grace alone," also "by faith alone."
That is what both the Scriptures and the Reformation
teach. Not love nor hope, but only faith justifies a life.
Faith alone, indeed, sets life upon a new foundation and
it is this new foundation alone that justifies it, so that I
can live before God. The foundation, however, is the life,
death, and resurrection of the Lord Jesus Christ. Without
this foundation a life cannot be justified before God. It is
left then to the mercy of death and damnation. Only by
living a life by the life, death, and resurrection of Jesus
Christ can we be justified before God. But faith means
finding and standing firm upon this foundation, to be
anchored in it and thereby to be held firm by it. Faith
means establishing one's life upon a foundation outside
one's own self, upon an eternal and holy foundation,

which is Christ. Faith means to be captivated by the glance of Jesus Christ, to see nothing other than him, to be torn out of imprisonment in one's own ego, to be set free by Jesus Christ. Faith is letting this action take place, which is an action in itself, but these two are not enough to explain the mystery. Only faith is certain, all else is doubt. Jesus Christ himself is the certainty of faith. I believe that my life is justified in the Lord Jesus Christ. There is no other way to the justification of my life than by faith alone. But faith is never alone, because where the true presence of Christ is, there is always with him, love and hope. It would be a false faith, a fanciful faith, a do-it-yourself invention, which could never justify a life, if there were no love or hope with it. It would be a learning by rote of sentences from the creeds, a dead faith, which did not include works of repentance and love. Not for a moment can faith and evil intentions live side by side. What happens to the human being in justification is all given, only faith is needed. When the person encounters Christ, all that Christ is becomes that person's own, but justification in my life is made my own by Christ, never by what I would want him to make of me. So, the heavens are rent asunder and the joyful message of God's salvation through Jesus Christ rings out in joyful sound from heaven to earth and the human race looks up and believes, and in believing receives Christ and, with him, everything. He lives before God!

Before that, he never knew in advance what life would be. He did not understand himself. The only way that he could seek to understand himself or justify his life was by his own limited possibilities and what he accomplished. In this way he justified himself by his own standards and before a self-made God. The possibilities and accomplishments of the living God were inaccessible to him, a life apart from these possibilities and activities of God was incomprehensible. A life which is based on a different foundation, a power that comes from a difference source, a help that comes from beyond him, was strange and remote. He could only find this kind of life when Christ justified him in his way. He lost his own life in Christ, now Christ becomes his life. " . . . I no longer live, but Christ lives in me" (Galatians 2:20).

We said at the beginning that the act of justification of a sinner is an ultimate or last thing. That was meant in the strongest sense. God's compassion with a sinner, can and must be heard as God's last word, or it will not be heard at all. The ultimacy of this word contains a double meaning: qualitatively, by its content, it is ultimate. There is no word of God which goes beyond his word of grace. There is nothing greater than a life justified before God. This word of God is a total break with all that went before, a break with the penultimate, not the natural or necessary end of the way that leads up to it, but rather God's judgment and condemnation of what went before.

It is God's free word, not the consequence of any other than God's own will, and therefore it is God's last word and the ultimate reality. It excludes any method of achieving justification in one's own way. There is no Lutheran or Pauline method of achieving the final word. Neither the way of Paul, who glorified in the Law and became an enemy of Christ, nor the way of Luther in the monastery where failure of the Law led to despair, led either of them to justification by the final word. No! Quite the opposite, both ways led to ultimate judgment. It was the sinner Paul and the sinner Luther, but not their sins, who were justified by the grace of God, according to the will of Christ. The ultimate word was at the same time the judgment upon the penultimate ways and things before the last. The qualitative sense of the last word forbids us from the first to look upon the way of Luther or the way of Paul as a way that we must go. They are ways that are condemned. Strong words! We should no more tread the way of Luther than that of the woman taken in adultery, the thief on the cross, Peter disowning Christ, or Paul fighting against him. The qualitative sense of the last word excludes every method once and for all. The Word justifies by forgiving and only by forgiving. It is neither right nor meaningful to preach to a Christian congregation—as one often hears today—that each must become like Mary Magdalene, like poor Lazarus, like the thief on the cross, or one of these "minor characters" in the Gospels before one can hear the ultimate Word of God. These attempts to explain the finality of the Word of God only succeed in undermining it. The content of the Christian message is not that one should become like one of the biblical characters, but to be like Christ himself. We are led to this, not by a method, but by faith alone. Otherwise, the gospel loses its value, its worth. Costly grace becomes cheap.

The justifying Word of God is, however, also in temporal terms, the final Word. There is something which comes before or leads up to that moment in time when the Word is spoken and heard—activity, suffering, progress, rising up, asking, hoping—a very serious span of time, whose end comes. Justification can only take place when the time is ready and the sinner stands under judgment. It is a time when the creature is aware of being guilty. Not every time is a time of grace, but now, precisely now, definitively now, is the "day of salvation" (2 Corinthians 6:2). The time of grace, "the day of salvation," is the last word in the sense that it is never possible for there to be a further word which goes beyond this word in the future. There is a time while God permits, waits, prepares, and there is a last time when the things before the last come to an end and are broken off. Luther must experience the monastery, Paul must go through his passion for the keeping of the Law, the thief must, through guilt, endure the cross, in order at last to hear the final word. A way must be trodden, the long way of the things before the last must be endured, each must sink under the burden of these things onto his knees—and yet the last word is not the crowning of this way, but the total break with it. In the face of the last word, Luther and Paul are no different from the thief on the cross. There must be a path to be walked, although this path comes to an end—that is the point at which God sets its end. That which comes before the last word remains necessary, but is in no way a path to the final goal and has no power to reach it.

The justifying grace of God can never be displaced from its position as the last word; it can never be simply the end of a journey, because it could as well be at the beginning as at the end; it is never the end of a way from the penultimate to the ultimate. The Word remains irreversibly ultimate, otherwise it would be predictable, reduced to a product and robbed of its divine nature. Grace would become cheap. It would not be a gift. [7]

The Prison Writings

On April 5, 1943, Bonhoeffer was arrested and taken to the old prison in Tegel, Berlin. He was placed in a cold and filthy cell and briefly in the solitary confinement ward, where those condemned to death were being held.

A few days later, he was handcuffed and driven to the Reich War Court. It was a military court, because of his membership of the Abwehr, but officials from the Central Security office were also present. Back in Tegel, he was held in a cell on the third floor, but later transferred to Cell 92 on the first floor, because of the risk of bombing raids. Conditions improved greatly for him. He was eventually able to write letters, and receive books and visitors. For eighteen months he was in Tegel and took every opportunity to continue his studies and think through the meaning of what was happening to him, his country, and his church.

On October 8, 1944, he was taken to the detention centre in the cellar of the Reich Central Security Office building on Prinz-Albrecht-Strasse. The interrogation was continued there from October 1944 to January 1945. Now there was no regular communication with his family or his fiancée, Maria von Wedemeyer, to whom he had been engaged on January 17, 1943. In Tegel, he had a continuous correspondence with family and friends. It was the 1953 publication in English of these letters, especially those to Eberhard Bethge, which drew attention to the radical development of his theology in prison. This was popularized ten years later in a bestseller paperback, *Honest to God* by John A.T. Robinson. The effect on theological thinking in the English-speaking world was dramatic.

Very little correspondence came out of Prinz-Albrecht-Strasse, but his last poem written in haste for his mother's birthday on December 28, 1944 reached her via his fiancée. It is still the most popular of his poems and has found its way into hymn books in many languages.

The Allied Armies advancing from east and west upon Berlin and their heavy bombing, led to his removal from Prinz-Albrecht-Strasse, together with other senior prisoners to a succession of prisons, concentration camps, and emergency buildings until his execution in Flossenbürg in the early hours of April 9, 1945.

Sermons and Letters

There were two sermons during his imprisonment; one in Tegel on the occasion of the marriage of his friend Eberhard Bethge to Bonhoeffer's own niece, Renate Schleicher (May 1943), and the other for the baptism of their first child (May 1944). A third sermon was to his fellow prisoners in an emergency prison en route to Flossenbürg. We do not have the script, but his texts were: "Praise be to the God and Father of our Lord Jesus Christ! In his great mercy he has given us new birth into a living hope through the resurrection of Jesus Christ from the dead" (1 Peter 1:3) and "By his wounds we are healed" (Isaiah 53:5).

These were the preaching texts in the Lutheran calendar for this Sunday after Easter.

Bethge reports from some of those prisoners who survived, that Bonhoeffer was reluctant to hold such a service until all requested it. He did not want to ambush Catholics with a Lutheran service, nor Kokorin, Molotov's nephew, an atheist. But all urged him. He explained the text and then "He spoke about the thoughts and decisions this captivity had produced in everyone. After this service the other prisoners wanted to smuggle Bonhoeffer over into their room so that he could hold a service there too. But it was not long before the door was opened and two civilians called out: 'Prisoner Bonhoeffer, get ready and come with us.'"[8] He knew what this meant. A summary trial and then he was executed by hanging. His last words were, "This is the end—for me the beginning of life."

The First Advent in Prison

Advent Sunday, November 28, 1943, was particularly poignant for Bonhoeffer. The Advent season was, for him, always an affair for family and friends and a time of almost childlike devotion. As he wrote letters from his lonely prison cell, he revealed more than nostalgia. He tried to come to terms with what was happening to him amidst the loneliness and the heavy bombing of Berlin.

To Eberhard Bethge, he wrote:

The first Sunday in Advent: it dawned after a quiet
night. In bed, I began looking for "our" Advent hymns
in the new hymnbook. There is hardly one of them which,
when I hum, does not take my mind back to Finkenwalde,
Schlönwitz, Sigurdshof (where Bonhoeffer and Bethge had
both sung these Advent hymns with their ordinands). Early
this morning when I had my morning devotions, I hung the
Advent "krantz" on a nail and fixed the Nativity scene by
Filippino Lippi on to it . . . How good it is that once again
you and Renate can celebrate Advent together! As I write,
you will be singing the first Advent hymns. When I think
of it, my mind conjures up the picture of the manger by
Altdorfer and the verse,

> The manger glows bright and clear,
> the very night gives out a light,
> darkness must not here appear,
> but faith remain both sure and bright.

—and then the Advent melody, not in 4/4 time, but with
a swinging rhythm, which fits the words.

The following day, after a very heavy air raid, he writes
again:

This Monday is clearly different from the usual Monday
atmosphere. We have been used to shouting and swearing in
the gangways, always at their worst on Monday mornings.

The experiences of the past week have quieted the loudest shouter and the bullies are subdued. The change is remarkable.

I must say something quite personal to you: during heavy bombing, especially last night, when the landmine fell on a nearby factory and windows were blown out, bottles and medicines burst out from the cupboards and fell on the floor in the dark, and there seemed no hope of getting out, I found myself driven back to prayer and the Bible. We must talk about this later. In more than one way this imprisonment is a very healthy, if drastic, cure! But leave the details until I am able to talk with you personally. [9]

Writing to his parents on the same day, the Altdorfer picture is again referred to, with his thoughts about its relevance:

Although I am not at all clear about whether, or, how, letters get to you, I want to write on this afternoon of Advent Sunday: Remember the Altdorfer Christmas scene, in which the Holy Family is depicted with the manger amidst the ruins of a broken down house—how could he, four hundred years ago, against all the traditions of his time, show the scene like that? It is really contemporary. We can, and should also, celebrate Christmas despite the ruins around us. Did he mean to say that to his contemporaries? It certainly speaks to us in this way today. I think of you as you now sit together with the children and with all the

Advent decorations — as in earlier years you did with us. We must do all this, even more intensively because we do not know how much longer we have. [10]

Second Sunday in Advent, December 5, 1943

He begins this Sunday with a desire to spend a quiet Sunday morning talking with his friend Eberhard Bethge. He gives to him the product of his solitary thinking:

To Eberhard Bethge:

I notice that my thoughts and ideas are tending more and more towards the Old Testament, so that I have been reading the Old Testament more than the New over these past few months. It is only when one knows that the names of God cannot be expressed, that one can express the name Jesus Christ; it is only when one so loves life and this world that the thought of losing them appears to be the end, that one can believe in the resurrection of the dead and a new world; it is only when one submits to the law of God, that one may really speak of grace; and only when one is convinced that the anger and vengeance of God against his enemy is justified, that forgiveness and love of our enemy can begin to move our hearts. The one who wants to go too quickly and directly to the New Testament for his guidance is in my opinion not a Christian. We have so often spoken about this and every day convinces me that it is true. One cannot, and may not, speak the last word before the penultimate word. We live in the penultimate and believe in the Last Word. Is that not so? Lutherans (so-called) and pietists would be shocked at this, but it's true all the same. In "The Cost of Discipleship" (chapter 1) I gave some indication of this, but I hadn't thought it through, then or later. That I have still to do. The consequences are very far reaching, among others, for the Catholic problem, for the concept of hierarchy, for the use of the Bible, etc., but above all, for ethics. Why is it that in the Old Testament, unashamedly and often to the glory of God, they lie (I've checked the references) murder, deceive, steal, commit adultery, and even go whoring (see the genealogy of Jesus); they have their doubts, curse, and blaspheme? And yet there is nothing of this in the New Testament? "Primitive" religion?—that is too naïve, because it is one and the same God. That's enough for the time being—we must talk about it. [11]

On December 15, 1943, Bonhoeffer wrote a long letter to Bethge, who had just returned to his unit at Lissa, Italy. Eberhard Bethge was now married to Renate and Bonhoeffer was aware that, had things been different, he might be about to marry Maria. There was a similarity in these two engagements which seemed to bring the two men closer together. Both were to much younger girls and they were both sensitively aware of the problems:

When I read your letter yesterday, it was a spring
bubbling up, a source without which my spiritual life would
wither and die. After a long drought, the first drop of water.
That must seem exaggerated talk to you, who meanwhile
have found another source and, apart from that, have
many possibilities for substitutes. In my solitude it is quite
different. I must live from what I can drain out of the past.
For me the future with Maria lies more in ideas of what is
on the horizon of hope, rather than in the realm of concrete
plans.

Bonhoeffer continues in this vein and then breaks off
suddenly to write as though he were sitting around the
fire with Eberhard, as they used to do. He recalls old dis-
cussions and then adds:

And finally, I must begin to tell you that, despite all
I have written in my letters, it is disgusting here. My
gruesome experiences often follow me into the darkness
of the night, and I can only combat them by repeating
innumerable hymns. One can accustom oneself to physical
hardship and for months ignore the body—too much in
fact—but the psychological burdens are not so easy to throw
off. I feel that I am aging under the pressure of what I see
and hear. The world becomes sickening and boring to me.
You must be surprised at me talking like this when you
remember what I have been writing in my letters. You write

to encourage and say that I "bear it all so well." I ask myself often who I really am. Am I the man who squirms under these ghastly conditions and cries out with complaints or am I the man who disciplines himself to appear outwardly unaffected by these things? And perhaps persuades himself that he is at peace, content, and in control of himself. Is he playing a part as in a stage play, or not? What does this "posture" really mean? In short, one knows less and less about oneself and no longer cares. I have had my fill of psychology and I dislike all this searching of soul more and more. I believe, therefore, that that is why Stifter and Gotthelf have become so important to me. They are far more important than all this talk of self-knowledge. (Adalbert Stifter was a nineteenth-century novelist and poet, whom Bonhoeffer would not have thought much of in normal times). He wrote of everyday things that we take for granted, like a walk in the garden. Many in prison found the same.

When his family had at last found one of his novels, *Witiko*, and sent it to him, he responded in raptures. "For me it is one of the finest books I know. The purity of its style and character drawing gives one a quite rare and peculiar feeling of happiness."[12] About the same time he was recommending Jeremias Gottheld to Marie, naming "Berner Geist" as one she should read after Kierkegaard.

Fourth Sunday in Advent

To Eberhard Bethge

The thought that you are at liberty to celebrate your fifth wartime Christmas with Renate gives me a sense of peace and confidence in the future. You will celebrate well and joyfully—that pleases me—and after that, it will not be too long before you are once more together on leave in Berlin. Surely by Easter, we shall all be together in peace and what a celebration that will be!

Over the last few weeks, lines from a hymn have been going through my head:

> Brother let it go,
> all that pains you so,
> all that now you lack—
> I bring all things back.

What does this mean, "I bring all things back?" Surely, that nothing is lost. In Christ all is gathered up and kept, everything in a transformed state, purified, and set free from agonizing selfishness of desires. Christ brings all this back again, but in the form that God had intended it from the beginning, unstained by our sins. This teaching is derived from Ephesians 1:10, "to bring all things in heaven and on earth together under one head, even Christ" and developed by Irenaus. It is a wonderful and comforting thought. "God seeks out what has passed away" completes the vision. And no one has expressed this more simply, even childlike, than Paul Gerhardt in the words that he puts into the mouth of the Christ child lying in the manger, "I bring all things back again."

Perhaps in the coming weeks this verse will help you somewhat. I have also seen, in these days, as never before, the value for me of the hymn, "Ich steh an Deiner Krippe hier . . ." (Before thy manger, here I stand), another hymn by Paul Gerhardt. I hadn't thought very much of it before. One has to be a long time alone and read it meditatively in order to get the best out of it. Every word is so extraordinarily beautiful and full of feeling. It is a little cloistered and mystical, but not so much as to spoil it; apart from our usual "we," there is a place for "I" and "Christ," and what that means is never better expressed than in this hymn; except perhaps in Thomas à Kempis', *Imitatio Christi*, which I am now dipping into using the Latin edition (it is so much more beautiful in the Latin than in the German). As I read it I think on a melody from Shütz in the Augustinian, "O bone Jesu." Does not this passage in a very special way, with its ecstatic yearning and such pure devotion, also somewhat echo the "bringing back" of all earthly longings? "Bringing back" is not to be confused with "sublimation," "sublimation" is flesh (and pietistic?!). "Bringing back" is spirit, not in the "spiritualistic meaning" of communicating with the dead (which is also flesh), but "a new creation," by the Holy Spirit. I believe that this thought is also very important for us when we have to speak to people in relation to their death, "I make all things anew." That means that we cannot and should not bring it back ourselves, but let Christ give it to us. [At my funeral, I want the choir to sing "Eins Bitte ich vom Herren" (Shütz, "One thing I desire of the Lord, that I dwell in the House of the Lord forever")], and "Eile mich God zu erretten" [Shütz, the same piece, "Hasten to deliver me, O God; to help me, O Lord"], and "O bone Jesu." [13]

His Last Advent

Advent came while Bonhoeffer was in the more severe surroundings of the cellar in Prinz-Albrecht-Strasse. It was not possible to continue the relaxed life of Tegel. But there was a slightly more relaxed period about Advent time leading to Christmas. On December 19, 1944, he was able to write to his fiancée, Maria von Wedemeyer:

My dearest Maria,

I'm so glad to be able to write you a Christmas letter, and through you, to convey my love to my parents and my brothers and sisters, and to thank you all. Our homes will be very quiet at this time. But I have often found that the quieter my surroundings, the more vividly I sense my connection with you all. It's as if, in solitude, the soul develops organs of which we're hardly aware in everyday

life. So I haven't for an instant felt lonely and forlorn. You
yourself, my parents—all of you, including my friends and
students on active service—are my constant companions.
Your prayers and kind thoughts, passages from the Bible,
long-forgotten conversations, pieces of music, books—all
are invested with life and reality as never before. I live in a
great unseen realm of whose real existence I'm in no doubt.
The old children's song about the angels says, "two to cover
me, two to wake me," and we grown-ups are no less in need
than children of preservation, night and morning, by kindly,
unseen powers. So you mustn't think I'm unhappy. Anyway,
what do happiness and unhappiness mean? They depend so
little on circumstances and so much more on what goes on
inside us. I'm thankful every day to have you—you and all
of you—and that makes me happy and cheerful . . . We've
now been waiting for each other for almost two years,
dearest Maria. Don't lose heart! [14]

In that letter he says he encloses "another few verses,"
as "his Christmas greeting to you, my parents, and my
brothers and sisters." It was his last poem:

By kindly powers surrounded, peaceful and true,
wonderfully protected with consolation dear,
safely, I dwell with you this whole day through
and surely into another year.

Though from the old our hearts are still in pain,
while evil days oppress with burdens still,

Lord, give to our frightened souls again,
salvation, and thy promises fulfill.

And should'st thou offer us the bitter cup, resembling
sorrow, filled to the brim and overflowing,
we will receive it thankfully, without trembling,
from thy hand so good and ever-loving.

But if it be thy will again to give
joy of this world and bright sunshine,
then in our minds we will past times relive
and all our days be wholly thine.

Let candles burn, both warm and bright,
which to our darkness thou hast brought,
and, if that can be, bring us together in the light,
thy light shines in the night unsought.

When we are wrapped in silence most profound,
may we hear that song most fully raised
from all the unseen world that lies around
and thou art by all thy children praised.

By kindly powers protected wonderfully,
confident, we wait for come what may.
Night and morning, God is by us, faithfully
and surely at each new born day. [15]

There is little doubt that among those "kindly powers" were his family and friends, but also that great "unseen realm of whose real existence" he was in no doubt. He had had a good life, full of joy and achievement. There had been agonizing times and suffering but he was sustained by music, conversations, and deep friendships within and without the family. The memory of these brought him nearer to that "great unseen realm" which he was soon to realize more clearly. At the end, he must have recalled his own poem, "Stages on the way to freedom," and especially its last stanza:

> *Come now, highest feast on the way to everlasting*
> *freedom,*
> *death. Lay waste the burdens of chains and walls*
> *which confine our earthly bodies and blinded souls,*
> *that we see at last what here we could not see.*
> *Freedom, we sought you long in discipline, action, and*
> *suffering.*
> *Dying, we recognize you now in the face of God.*[16]

It was the end on April 9, 1945, but for him, "the beginning of life."

Notes and Sources

Introduction

1. Clyde Fant, *Bonhoeffer*: *Worldly Preaching* (Nashville: Thomas Nelson, 1975), 134.
2. Eberhard Bethge, *Dietrich Bonhoeffer*: *A Biography* (Minneapolis: Fortress, 2000), 92.

Barcelona—March 1928–February 1929

1. Dietrich Bonhoeffer, *Werke*, Vol. 10, 20–21.
2. Ibid, 60.
3. Ibid, 112.
4. Ibid, 529–33.

The American Year—1929–1930

1. Bonhoeffer, *Werke*, Vol. 10, 26.
2. Dietrich Bonhoeffer, *Love Letters from Cell 92*, trans. John Brownjohn (New York: HarperCollins, 1996). 154.
3. Dietrich Bonhoeffer, *No Rusty Swords* (London: Collins, 1965), 109.
4, Bonhoeffer, *Werke*, Vol. 10, 582–87.
5. Edwin Robertson, ed. and trans., *Dietrich Bonhoeffer's Prison Poems* (Grand Rapids, Mich.: Zondervan: 2005), 89.

Berlin—1931–1933

1. Bonhoeffer, *Werke*, Vol. 14, 112–14.
2. Edwin Robertson, *Dietrich Bonhoeffer's Meditations on Psalms* (Grand Rapids, Mich.: Zondervan, 2005), 36–41.
3. Luke 12:42–46.

4. Bonhoeffer, *Werke*, Vol. 11, 385–94.
5. Ibid., Vol. 12, 431–33.

Berlin—1932–1933

1. Bonhoeffer, *Werke*, Vol. 11, 454–63.
2. Ibid., Vol. 12, 465–70.

London—1933–1935

1. Bethge, *Bonhoeffer*, 325–26.
2. Bethge, *Bonhoeffer*, 339.
3. Bonhoeffer, *Werke*, Vol. 13, 332–37.
4. Ibid, 338–43.

Finkenwalde—1935–1937

1. Bethge, *Bonhoeffer*, 412–413.
2, Bonhoeffer, *Werke*, Vol. 14, 911–18.
3. Ibid, 920–925.

Collective Pastorates—1938–1940

1. Bonhoeffer, *Werke*, Vol. 14, 593–94.
2. Ibid., 761–63.
3. Ibid., Vol. 15, 492–98.

War—Conspiracy—Prison—Death—1939–1945

1. Bethge, *Bonhoeffer*, 681.
2. Bonhoeffer, *Werke*, Vol. 8, 236.
3. Ibid., 17–39. Also, *Letters and Papers from Prison*, (SCM Press, Enlarged Edition, 1971), 3–17.
4. Bonhoeffer, *Werke*, Vol. 15, 537–43.
5. Bonhoeffer, *Werke*, Vol. 8. Also, *Ethics* (SCM Press).
6. Bethge, *Bonhoeffer*, 860–61.
7. Bonhoeffer, *Werke*, Vol 15, 492–98.
8. Bethge, *Bonhoeffer*, 926–27.
9. Bonhoeffer, *Werke*, Vol 8, 212–15 (selected passages).

10. Ibid., 218.
11. Ibid., 226–27.
12. Ibid., 232–35.
13. Ibid., 245–48.
14. Bonhoeffer, *Love Letters from Cell 92*, 227–228, first paragraph.
15. Bonhoeffer, *Werke*, Vol. 8, 607–8. Also, Robertson, *Dietrich Bonhoeffer's Prison Poems*.
16. Ibid., 570–572. Also, Robertson, *Dietrich Bonhoeffer's Prison Poems*.

Dietrich Bonhoeffer's Meditations on Psalms

Editor and Translator
Edwin Robertson

A one-volume collection of legendary author Dietrich Bonhoeffer's profound and influential meditations on the Psalms, previously untranslated. Eloquent, incisive, encouraging, challenging, Bonhoeffer invites us to find in the Psalms both a path toward rest in God and a call to Christ-like living as followers of the Lord Jesus.

Hardcover: 0-310-26703-X

Pick up a copy today at your favorite bookstore!

Dietrich Bonhoeffer's Prison Poems

Editor and Translator
Edwin Robertson

This book contains the power-ful, personal, and deeply mov-ing poetry written by Dietrich Bonhoeffer, one of the most important Christian writers and martyrs of the century. From his prison cell, where he awaited execution for conspiring to assassinate Adolf Hitler, Bonhoeffer wrote ten powerful poems, charged with the white-hot emotions and disarming candor of a man who lived and ultimately died by the truth.

Hardcover: 0-310-26704-8

Pick up a copy today at your favorite bookstore!

ZONDERVAN™

GRAND RAPIDS, MICHIGAN 49530 USA

WWW.ZONDERVAN.COM